we

THE IDEAL CUSTOMER RELATIONSHIP

Steve Yastrow

SelectBooks, Inc.
New York, New York

WE: The Ideal Customer Relationship

This edition published by SelectBooks, Inc. For information address SelectBooks, Inc., One Union Square West, New York, New York 10003

First Edition

ISBN 978-1-59079-121-9

Library of Congress Cataloging-in-Publication Data

Yastrow, Steve, 1959-
    We : the ideal customer relationship / by Steve Yastrow. -- 1st ed.
        p. cm.
    ISBN-13: 978-1-59079-121-9 (hardbound : alk. paper)
    ISBN-10: 1-59079-121-5
    1. Customer relations. 2. Customer services. 3. Relationship marketing.
I. Title.
    HF5415.5.Y37 2007
    658.8'12--dc22
                                2006102595

All real living is meeting.

—MARTIN BUBER
I and Thou

CONTENTS

one

WHY WE?   1

The Essential Question   1
Think "We"   2
You Can Create We Relationships   3
Relationship: From "Us & Them" to "We"   4
Marketing Teaches Us the Wrong Things About Marketing   28
"I and Thou"—Seeing an Old Idea in a New Light   30
From Experience to Engagement   32

two

ENCOUNTERS: THE BUILDING BLOCKS OF WE RELATIONSHIPS   37

Transactions vs. Encounters   37
At the Crossroads of We: 41
The Three Elements of a We Encounter
Encounter Element #1: Engagement in the Moment   42
Encounter Element #2: Conversation   73
Encounter Element #3: Uniqueness   89
The Encounter's Afterglow: The Feeling of "With"   120

three

FROM ENCOUNTER TO RELATIONSHIP: THE ONGOING CONVERSATION   123

A Relationship Forms from a Continuity of Encounters   124
Memory Is the Connection Between Encounters   125
The Rhythm of Encounter—Building Momentum   134
in Your Relationship
The Mix of Moments—Milestones and Bridges   140
The Continuity of Encounters Becomes   147
an Ongoing Conversation

four

THE CONTINUITY DEVELOPS: REVEALING THE WAY WE COMPLEMENT EACH OTHER   157

Complementary Understanding, Goals, Actions, Outcomes   160

Complementary Understanding: We Know Each Other in Relation to Ourselves   161

Complementary Goals: We Believe that What Is Good for One Is Good for the Other   170

Complementary Actions: We Do Things that Are Mutually Reinforcing   177

Complementary Outcomes: We Both Benefit from Each Other's Success   181

five

WE AMONG MANY: RELATIONSHIPS BETWEEN ORGANIZATIONS   187

Organizational Relationships Are Built from Individual Relationships   187

Ensure that Employees Understand How to Create We Relationships   190

Ensure that Employees Can Create We Relationships   194

Many of Them, Many of You   198

CONCLUSION: WE—THE BENEFITS ENDURE   201

Our Shared Future—What's Next Matters as Much as What Is   201

ACKNOWLEDGMENTS   203

INDEX   207

WHY WE?

The Essential Question

WHEN THINKING OF THEIR RELATIONSHIP
WITH YOU ...
HOW MANY OF YOUR CUSTOMERS
THINK "WE"

HOW MANY OF YOUR CUSTOMERS
THINK "US AND THEM"?

THINK "WE"

> How do you want your customers to think about you and/or your organization?
>
> Do you want them to see you in the distance…as "Them?"
>
> Or, do you want your customers to think of themselves and you as closely interrelated…as "We?"

Consider the difference. All of your customers, whether they represent themselves as consumers or buy on behalf of a business, live rich, full, colorful lives. From the moment they wake up in the morning until they fall asleep at night, their thoughts are engaged in the business of life. Things to do, people to speak with, questions to be answered, decisions to be made. For most people life is enjoyable, for nearly everyone it is crowded. Your customers' brains are active all day, processing a series of thought-stories that capture the present, reflect on the past, and anticipate the future. They are continuously interrupted with too many sensory inputs, and they are constantly defending themselves against these interruptions; after all, the human brain is amazing, but it can handle only so much.

It is a privilege to enter this stream of consciousness and be noticed by your customer. Moreover, it is difficult to enter this stream of consciousness. Consider, also, that your customer himself is an actor in most of the thought-stories going on in his brain; every person is the center of his own universe. You have a much better chance of participating in those stories if he thinks of you as interrelated with him, as "We," than if he sees you in the distance, as "Them."

It is both possible and worthwhile to strive for this feeling of "We."

> **Relationships have become POWERFUL differentiators.**

As an advisor to companies in varied industries, I've watched many customer-driven trends evolve over the years. I saw how discerning customers began to look well beyond the promises that companies make in their marketing campaigns and started to consider the entire set of experiences that they have with a company. This is a subject I explore in depth in my first book, *Brand Harmony*. Lately, I've seen that customers are looking not only beyond marketing promises when making purchase decisions, but also looking beyond the products themselves. Customers see products as relatively interchangeable. So what do customers see as different?

What I have learned through my experience is this: Relationships have become *powerful* differentiators. Customers can't tell if your product is better than your competitor's product, but they *can* tell if they have a better relationship with you than with your competitor.

If relationships are such powerful differentiators, what is the most productive, profitable, and sustainable customer relationship?

The We relationship.

In a We relationship, you each think less about what separates you and more about what intertwines you.

In contrast, if your customer's view of your relationship is not "We" but "Us & Them," he will focus more on what he can get from you—and on what he believes you get from him—and less on how you collaborate to reach your goals together.

YOU CAN CREATE WE RELATIONSHIPS

Although it is ultimately up to your customers to decide if they want to enter into a We relationship with you, there are many things you can do to invite them in. You cannot control your customers, but you can control many of the factors that encourage a We relationship. This is true in all business relationships, whether they are between individuals or groups.

This book is about creating We relationships with customers and enjoying the benefits of those relationships. This is within your reach. Now.

RELATIONSHIP: FROM "US & THEM" TO "WE"

The Frame of Reference Is the Relationship

Consider what most companies measure. They track product releases; they commemorate new store openings; they calculate revenues, profits, and number of transactions. But most companies do not measure the quality of the relationships they have with customers.

Now, consider what the customer is measuring. Think of a customer of a retail giant such as Macy's. He doesn't care about the amount of profit he's generating for the company. He doesn't care whether he is part of a high-priority target audience. What he *does* care about is how he is treated, whether they listen to him, whether they notice his wants and needs, whether they work with him or against him. In essence, he cares about the quality of the relationship he has with the company.

What would happen if companies focused on the same measure that customers are focused on, relationships?

> My client and I are eating lunch in a hotel restaurant. He is a senior executive of the company that owns and manages this hotel. It is a beautiful restaurant, with a unique and diverse menu, overlooking a warm, inviting lobby that could win interior design awards. But the real success of this company is not in menus or lobbies, it is in the way they create relationships with customers. I say, "If I were your competitor, I could walk into this hotel and copy your interior design, menus, pricing, brochures. What I could not copy are the personal relationships you have with your customers. Duplicating those relationships would be impossible for me."

Competitors can copy much of what you do, but they cannot copy the rich, interesting, private relationships you have with customers. Establishing strong customer relationships is the best competitive strategy. They are unique to you and your customer, and make you look unique in the customer's eyes.

If you were to listen in on conversations going on in most companies, whether they are conversations in the marketing department, the boardroom, or among the operations team, you wouldn't hear much about relationships with individual customers. Even companies with formal efforts involving extensive Customer Relationship Management (CRM) systems most often use those systems to enhance discrete transactions, not to build long-term relationships. Those companies that do focus on building strong customer relationships, as a primary, daily company effort, are the exception, not the rule.

> **Relationships are the best competitive strategy.**

Why is the building of customer relationships such a low priority for so many companies?

Progress Has Led Us Astray

For thousands of years commerce was very low-tech, with every sale requiring significant human intervention and attention. Over the last 100 years, thousands of technological advances have helped companies increase their sales while reducing labor. From Henry Ford's Model T assembly line to network advertising, and on to the latest customer database management software, marketers and sellers have acquired new means to sell more products to more customers with less effort.

This progress created a boon for companies. It allowed them to get big while delegating the work of humans to less expensive, and frequently more productive, non-human tools. In much the same way that the hand-crafting of products evolved into mass manufacturing, the traditions of one-on-one selling that had been at the heart of commerce for 8,000 years evolved into mass advertising. It is no longer necessary to make every product by hand, and it is also no longer necessary to make every sale "by hand." Media outlets and computers can handle much of the messy work of customer inter-actions for businesses.

The result of this ability to delegate customer interactions—to computers, marketing communications, distributors, etc.—is that companies have found it convenient to hold customers at a dis-tance. This would have meant sure bankruptcy in the past, but now many of our most powerful technologies have given companies an excuse to depersonalize their customer relationships.

> **The choice with technology & customers is clear: Will you use technology as a way to get closer to customers, or will you use it as a way to avoid customers?**

Understand that I am not taking an anti-tech-nology stance; I am not a technophobe. Remem-ber that guy in the '80s who walked onto the airplane loaded like a techie-packhorse with his bag phone and enormous laptop? That was me. In the early '90s, to the chagrin of Hyatt Corpora-tion's legal and IT departments, I took a chance and launched the first website for a major hotel company. I always bought the smallest (newest) cell phone and the fastest (newest) computer. I think it's great that technology affords us major conveniences like ATMs, booking travel online, and the electronic singing toothbrush.

However, I am observing that companies often use technology to avoid being close to their customers. Companies usually don't insti-tute these technology-driven changes for the benefit of the customer—they do it for their own interests. There is nothing about an automated call-prompting system *("Please say or touch your 16-digit credit card number")* that is good for customers.

The choice with technology and customers is clear. Will you use technology as a way to get closer to customers, or will you use it as a way to avoid customers?

An experience I had a few years ago highlights this kind of choice:

> For years, I had two near-identical taxi choices for traveling between my house and Chicago's O'Hare Airport. I could call either American Taxi or 303 Taxi, and a cab would arrive in minutes to take me to or from the airport. They

seemed so interchangeable that I would often call both of them at the same time from different phones and award the business to whoever answered the phone first.

Then, about ten years ago, both companies made investments in technologies that affected the customer experience. American Taxi invested in an automated telephone reservations service, requiring customers to press a series of buttons before talking to a reservations agent. I had to type "1" to distinguish that I was a passenger and not a package, "1" again to indicate that I was paying with cash or credit card as opposed to a corporate account, "1" again if I was at home or "2" if I was at the airport, and then I had to enter my 10-digit phone number. I'm sure this innovation reduced labor costs at their dispatch center, since I was now doing the data entry work previously done by their people.

The 303 Taxi company elected instead to make a technological investment inside their taxis; they implemented an automated dispatch service that sent assignments to a screen on each cab's dashboard. This had a noticeable impact on the customer experience, since the least pleasant part of riding with both companies had been listening to dispatchers shouting instructions to drivers. My rides were always punctuated with cries such as "Cab 73, why haven't you picked up your fare at Terminal 2 yet?" and "Cab 27, you haven't responded to me yet!" even though I was in cab 58. I had complained to both companies about this cacophony, and they both admitted to me that this was a common customer complaint. But suddenly, 303 cabs became quiet. American Taxi rides, however, were still an opportunity to listen to dispatchers scolding drivers.

Contrast the choices these two companies made. American Taxi invested in technology that made their processes more efficient. 303 invested in technology that made the cab ride more pleasant. (Their automated dispatch system may have also had the collateral benefit of being more efficient.) I immediately shifted all my business to 303.

Examples of using technology to support customer relationships are not uncommon. I'm sure you can think of many of them. But unfortunately, most companies choose the route American Taxi has taken. I was very frustrated this morning waiting on hold for a British Airways reservations agent. I tried to book a flight on their website, but I repeatedly got a strange error. So I called their 800 number and was forced to listen to interminably long, repeating, recorded raves about how great it is to book on ba.com, and that I'd be paying $20 per ticket extra for the pleasure of speaking to a real live person. They clearly look at their website as a way to reduce costs, not as a way to make my experience better.

Another example:

> I switched from a Dell computer to an Apple Macintosh computer for many reasons, but I remember very clearly the moment that helped me make the decision. When I was a Dell customer, I always considered a call to their tech support line a very unpleasant experience. I had to navigate a labyrinthine phone system, wait interminably on hold, and, if I ended up with the wrong support group, I had to go back into a long queue. One day while I was waiting on hold I remembered an article that described Dell's innovative inventory management system. Apparently, their system is so advanced that Dell is able to keep their entire spare parts inventory in an unimaginably small room. Suddenly, the irony struck me: Although they've created the most efficient inventory system in the world, reducing their costs for overhead and labor to the absolute minimum, I have to run a tiresome obstacle course every time I want help with the broken computer they sold me. It doesn't add up.

It doesn't have to be this way. Technology can be used to get closer to customers. If I want to talk to an Apple tech support person, I can go to apple.com and make a reservation with a "genius" (tech support rep) at my local Apple Store and know that he'll be waiting for me when I arrive. /

Another excellent example of using technology to get closer to customers is the customized recommendations on Netflix, which are based on a member's past movie orders. Nearly half of a new film's budget can go to marketing, such as mass advertising and promotional efforts. Like most advertising, many of these messages are lost in the noise of daily life—they aren't noticed by their intended audience. However, the films that are advertised to me on Netflix are specially chosen for me, based on who I am. As Chris Anderson points out in *The Long Tail*, Netflix shows me my own personal billboard. Think of the difference. I see traditional movie advertising as trying to "sell" me something I might want, but I see Netflix as collaborating with me to help me find what I really want. They've made the advertising about *me*, not just about the movies they are trying to sell.

The Long Tail is chock full of examples of companies using technology to build stronger relationships with customers. As Anderson describes, lists of books that sell in a Barnes & Noble store or records that sell in a Tower Records store are not a true gauge of what people want to buy; they reflect only what people want to buy from the limited inventory available. Anderson demonstrates that when these inventory and shelf space constraints are taken away in an online environment, the top-selling hits make up a smaller portion of the sales. For example, he writes, the bottom 1.2 million books in sales rank account for only 1.7 percent of sales at Barnes & Noble stores, but a full 10 percent of online sales at their website. If given a broader choice, people find what they want, and they do not have to settle for what the stores keep in stock. Provide customers with a *good* technology tool—for example, a good website with great search capacity—and you will give your customers the experience they need.

Despite these positive examples, my experience shows that companies will more often make the wrong choice. The choices made by American Taxi, British Airways, and Dell are the rule, not the exception. As companies hide behind technology in the interest of efficiency, it is harder for customers to get personalized attention from sellers than it has ever been before.

The result? We feel frustrated with the relationships we have with many of the companies that sell things to us. We love having cell phones, but we hate our cell phone carriers. We love to travel across the country, but we dread the process of flying on a major airline. We like to watch TV, but we hate waiting home all day for the cable guy.

In short, we no longer believe that many of the companies we patronize are on our side. Our relationships feel adversarial. It's "Us vs. Them."

Companies have depersonalized their customers, and they have come to think of acquiring customers the same way a trawling fisherman approaches a school of fish—"Drop enough nets in the right places, and we're sure to snag a few." Modern advertising-based marketing fuels this belief. It teaches us that the best way to sell to customers is through brute force: "If you manage to expose your customer to enough powerful sales and marketing messages, the customer will submit and want to buy from you." Even salespeople, who throughout the ages won business through relationships, often follow this advertising-influenced model. They talk about "getting enough at-bats with the customer," "having an elevator pitch," and "attacking target markets."

If this way of looking at marketing and selling works for your business, have at it. (If you feel this way and you're reading this while standing in the aisle of a bookstore, don't buy this book.) However, most companies would be better off—and their customers would be better off—if they thought less about "getting their name out in the marketplace" and "cutting through the clutter" and more about creating relationships that are sustainable, productive, and profitable.

Although companies can enjoy significant benefits from the efficiencies afforded by modern technology, they often pay a bigger price by distancing themselves from the customer. Where is the real payoff? Short-term savings in efficiency, or the long-term benefit of strong customer relationships?

Relationships Evolve

The boundary that divides you & your customer transforms into the relationship that defines you.

Every relationship with a customer starts off, inherently, at a distance. After all, you don't know each other, and love-at-first-sight is typically not a feature of business relationships.

In distant relationships, each individual thinks more in terms of himself than he does in terms of the relationship. Like the gravitational force between two distant planets, the relationship between them at this distance exerts very little pull.

As your relationship with your customer develops and you come closer together, the customer will not only see how you relate to him, but also how your joint relationship benefits him. The boundary that divided you and your customer is now transformed into the relationship that defines you and your customer.

If this becomes a truly great relationship, the customer will spend less time focusing on you as a distinct, separate entity, and more time focusing on the entity that you comprise together, i.e., your relationship. He will not think "Us & Them." He will think "We."

We vs. Us & Them

Us & Them

Relationship: The amount of business you do together can go up or down with no warning.

"YOU CAN HAVE A SUCCESSFUL BUSINESS WITH 'US & THEM,' BUT YOUR SUCCESS IS TREMENDOUSLY LIMITED. AND WHEN YOU HAVE THAT 'WE' RELATIONSHIP, IT OPENS UP THE DOOR FOR POTENTIAL OPPORTUNITIES, AND THE ABILITY AND PERMISSION TO TELL YOUR CUSTOMER ABOUT NEW AND INNOVATIVE THINGS, WHICH YOU'RE GOING TO HAVE TO DO IF YOU'RE GOING TO KEEP CREATING AND RECREATING YOUR BUSINESS."—**DOUG DUCEY, CEO, Cold Stone Creamery**

We relationships offer much more potential than Us & Them relationships. An Us & Them relationship is driven by price, convenience, quality of service, and product. Your customer sees you as a provider of a product or service, and the relationship is transactional. An Us & Them customer is often low maintenance, allowing you to do business with relatively little effort. However, an Us & Them relationship is essentially unpredictable; the amount of business your customer does with you can go up or down without warning.

A We relationship is substantially different from an Us & Them relationship. A We customer sees the relationship as collaborative and mutual; he thinks "We" when thinking about himself and your company. This customer sees your company as unique and, therefore, not interchangeable with the competition. And you see the needs of each We customer as distinct from the needs of all other customers. You go beyond using each other to accomplish things and actually see your relationship as one in which you do things together. A We customer often requires more effort and attention than an Us & Them customer. However, this customer will also put more personal effort into the relationship. In a We relationship, you communicate your needs and desires well to each other, and you are more likely to know where you stand with each other. ⟶

> **We**
> Relationship:
> You know,
> at all times,
> where you
> stand with
> each other.

Why We Is More Profitable

"MAN'S WILL TO PROFIT AND TO BE POWERFUL HAVE THEIR NATURAL AND PROPER EFFECT SO LONG AS THEY ARE LINKED WITH, AND UPHELD BY, HIS WILL TO ENTER IN RELATION."—**MARTIN BUBER,** *I AND THOU*

We relationships are certainly a better way to live. Adversarial, transactional relationships are draining. Whether they are with customers, colleagues, vendors, or bureaucrats, We relationships rejuvenate and energize you in ways that adversarial relationships cannot.

However, the value of We is greater than the impact of just feeling good. When your customers are in a We relationship with you, they want to be more involved with you. You also want to be

Differences Between a We Relationship & an Us & Them Relationship:

US & THEM RELATIONSHIP	WE RELATIONSHIP
Customer decisions are based on price, quality of service, and product.	Customer decisions are based on past history of doing business with you.
You are a product or a provider.	You are a collaborator.
You do things FOR your customer.	You do things WITH your customer.
You have similar relationships with other customers.	You have a unique relationship with this customer.
The amount of business you do together can go up or down without warning.	Your future is more predictable.
You each devote limited attention to the relationship.	You each are willing to devote substantial attention to the relationship.
The relationship's potential is limited.	The relationship's possibilities are boundless.

more involved with them. A We relationship reveals a world of new possibilities that can create profit for you *and* your customer.

In collaboration with my colleagues Steve Elliott and Caroline Ceisel, I conducted a study of 550 business travelers in order to determine if a strong relationship led to increased loyalty, increased purchases, and unsolicited referrals. I was trying to learn whether customers *want* relationships with companies with whom they do business. We deliberately designed questions to encourage responses that consider both personal and business purchase decisions.

● ON A VERY BASIC LEVEL, RESPONDENTS INDICATED THAT THEY PREFER TO HAVE RELATIONSHIPS WITH COMPANIES, AS OPPOSED TO JUST TRANSACTING BUSINESS WITH THOSE COMPANIES.

WOULD YOU RATHER BUY FROM A BUSINESS THAT...	
You have a relationship with?	**89%**
Simply provides you with the service or product when you need it?	**11%**

● PEOPLE ALSO WANT TO BE HEARD AND TO BE IN DIALOGUE WITH COMPANIES FROM WHOM THEY MAKE PURCHASES:

WOULD YOU RATHER BUY FROM A BUSINESS THAT...	
You have regular conversations with?	**86%**
Assumes they know what you need?	**14%**

> **WOULD YOU RATHER BUY FROM A BUSINESS THAT...**
>
> Talks to you about a future decision you might make? **90%**
>
> Talks to you about a decision you already made? **10%**

● ALTHOUGH PRICE IS IMPORTANT IN EVERY PURCHASE DECISION, PEOPLE WILL OFTEN LOOK TO A RELATIONSHIP AS A DECIDING FACTOR.

> **WHICH ARE YOU MORE LIKELY TO BUY FROM...**
>
> Businesses that have the best prices? **21%**
>
> Businesses you have a relationship with? **79%**

> **HOW DESIRABLE ARE...(SCALE OF 1-6)**
>
> Businesses that you have a relationship with? average **5.41** out of 6
>
> Businesses that have the best prices? average **4.60** out of 6

● PEOPLE ARE ALSO MORE LIKELY TO RECOMMEND COMPANIES WITH WHOM THEY HAVE RELATIONSHIPS THAN THOSE WITH THE BEST PRICES.

> **WHICH ARE YOU MORE LIKELY TO RECOMMEND TO OTHERS...**
>
> Businesses that have the best prices? **14%**
>
> Businesses you have a relationship with? **86%**

● HOWEVER, DESPITE THEIR DESIRE FOR GOOD RELATIONSHIPS, RESPONDENTS REPORT THAT THEY DON'T BELIEVE THEY HAVE RELATIONSHIPS WITH MOST OF THE COMPANIES THEY DO BUSINESS WITH.

DO YOU THINK YOU HAVE A RELATIONSHIP WITH MOST OF THE BUSINESSES THAT YOU BUY FROM?	
Yes	**38%**
No	**62%**

Our sample included past guests of Kimpton Hotels, a chain of 43 boutique hotels in the U.S. As shown in the next question, which was asked of these people, more respondents said they had a relationship with Kimpton than with other companies they purchased from. (We asked this question of Kimpton's past guests in another survey and received a similar response.)

DO YOU THINK YOU HAVE A RELATIONSHIP WITH KIMPTON HOTELS?	
Yes	**74%**
No	**26%**

Importantly, of those guests who say they have a relationship with Kimpton, 92 percent say that they stay at Kimpton Hotels more as a result of that relationship:

DO YOU BELIEVE YOU STAY WITH KIMPTON HOTELS MORE AS A RESULT OF THAT RELATIONSHIP?	
Yes	**92%**
No	**8%**

(Asked only of those who said "yes" to relationship with Kimpton.)

We also surveyed 1,500 customers of Cold Stone Creamery ice cream stores, and we asked them similar questions:

DO YOU THINK YOU HAVE A RELATIONSHIP WITH COLD STONE CREAMERY?	
Yes	**40%**
No	**60%**

DO YOU BELIEVE THAT YOU VISIT COLD STONE CREAMERY STORES MORE AS A RESULT OF THAT RELATIONSHIP?	
Yes	**84%**
No	**16%**

(Asked only of those who said "yes" to relationship with Cold Stone.)

Note that although fewer people consider themselves in a relationship with an ice cream store company than with a hotel company, Cold Stone Creamery customers who consider themselves in a relationship with the company do, in fact, visit their stores more as a result of that relationship.

In a parallel study conducted in cooperation with The List, Inc., of Atlanta, Georgia, we asked 257 executives about their relationships with their customers. After explaining the difference between We relationships and Us & Them relationships, we asked a number of questions to understand what value sellers felt they achieved due to these different kinds of relationships.

The results were surprising. One might assume that respondents would believe that having similar relationships with many customers would be desirable, because it would be lower in cost and more efficient. However, the results showed that people are willing to invest in higher maintenance, unique relationships with customers.

WOULD YOU RATHER HAVE...

Similar relationships with many customers (Us & Them)?	**9%**
Unique relationships with individual customers (We)?	**91%**

WOULD YOU RATHER HAVE...

Customers who are "low maintenance," but tend to increase or decrease the amount of business they do with you without warning?	**6%**
Customers who require more attention, but communicate their attitudes and intentions?	**94%**

Similarly, respondents to our study said they would rather have customers who look beyond the price of the transaction at hand and make purchase decisions based on the history of the relationship.

WOULD YOU RATHER HAVE...

Customers who fairly award their business based on the best price?	**9%**
Customers who award their business based on your past history of doing business with them?	**91%**

The reason respondents responded the way they did is explained by the following questions, which show that they believe We relationships to be more profitable and to generate more referrals.

WHICH CUSTOMER IS MORE PROFITABLE?

Us & Them?	5%
We?	95%

WHICH CUSTOMER IS MORE LIKELY TO RECOMMEND YOU TO OTHERS?

Us & Them?	3%
We?	97%

WHICH CUSTOMER WOULD YOU RATHER HAVE MORE OF?

Us & Them?	5%
We?	95%

HOW DESIRABLE ARE...(SCALE OF 1-6)

Us & Them customer relationships?	average **3.41** out of 6
We customer relationships?	average **5.62** out of 6

Although respondents said they believe We relationships are more profitable and desirable, they see many challenges to creating more We relationships. We asked these executives to comment on the challenges.

Many of the respondents described challenges related to learning enough about a customer to create a strong relationship with him:

> "Getting customers to open up to what they're really thinking and become transparent."

> "Client's willingness to initially share information about their needs and business at a deeper level."

> "Developing sufficient understanding of our clients' needs."

> "Not knowing our customers or the opportunities we could have with our customers."

Similarly, there is a challenge to getting a customer to understand the seller well enough:

> "Helping the customer or prospect see me as unique."

> "Not a lot of customers know what our company does, or they have a misconception about what we can provide or what we can do."

Both of these issues, understanding your customer and helping your customer understand you, will be discussed throughout this book, with special emphasis in Chapter 2, "Encounters—The Building Blocks of We Relationships," and Chapter 4, "The Continuity Develops: Revealing the Way We Complement Each Other."

A number of respondents described challenges related to turnover in the customer's organization.

> "Maintaining relationships with the constant change of customer personnel."

> "Managing through client personnel changes."

"Making sure the other 'We' does not move on to
another position."

In Chapter 5, "We Among Many: Relationships Between Organizations," we will discuss how to meet this challenge by ensuring that the relationship between two organizations is built on a number of strong We relationships between individuals.

Not surprisingly, many respondents identified challenges within their own organizations:

"Getting our sales staff to think We instead of Us and Them."

"Having all levels of staffing understand their role in
maintaining that relationship."

"Hiring and maintaining a staff that has the expertise required
to create and maintain strategic long-term relationships."

"'It's just a job' attitude has to be upgraded to 'my
job's important.'"

"We are a company that helps our clients build relationships
with their customers, but we don't always focus on the 'We'
with our clients. We get caught up in the here and now.
I believe that we lose sight of our own client relationships."

These issues will be discussed throughout the book, especially in Chapter 5, "We Among Many: Relationships Between Organizations."

We also heard about the challenge of finding goals in common with your customer:

"Finding the right fit...We relationships are built on both
partners sharing the same business goals."

"A challenge is when all they think about is the bottom line
now and not the bottom line in the future."

These issues will be addressed in Chapter 4, "The Continuity Develops: Revealing the Way We Complement Each Other," in a section on complementary goals.

Respondents also recognized the challenge of allocating time—both within their own organizations and with the customer—to building a relationship.

> "Having the time needed to develop the We relationships in the midst of day-to-day business pressures and time constraints."

> "Short attention spans. Relationships take time to develop and it's rare that that time is allocated anymore."

> "We relationships involve added focus and commitment; it's not about the one shot, it's all about the longer term connection."

Addressing these and other challenges to building We relationships is the focus of this book. However, facing these challenges is worth it; We relationships are more profitable, productive, and sustainable.

Your Brand Is Not About You: We Is the Best Brand Strategy

Who do your customers love more, you or themselves?

I have asked this question of thousands of workshop participants and numerous clients, and, to date, not one person has claimed his customers love him more than they love themselves. I doubt there is one executive in the country who would answer this question any differently.

> **A Reality of Life: No matter how much your customers love you, they love themselves more.**

But, if this is the case, why do companies spend so much time talking about themselves whenever they get their customers' attention? If customers care about sellers so little relative to how they care about themselves, why do those sellers insist on advertising their features and benefits as a way to attract customers?

One of the great fallacies of the modern practice of branding is the belief that customers actually care very much about what companies

> The strongest
> brands are
> not about
> products
> or services,
> they are
> about
> relationships.

are trying to sell. Relative to other things in their lives, the latest gadget doesn't rate very high. Billions of dollars are spent each year to advertise the newest model, the latest upgrade, and the biggest promotional offer, under the mistaken belief that customers are actually waiting around to hear these messages. Sure, many advertising messages work, but most don't. I'm convinced that the lion's share of advertising investments are a waste of money, and the main reason is that companies are trying to create compelling, memorable brands that are based only on themselves and their products.

In my consulting work, I often conduct market research to determine what most attracts—or annoys—customers. Traditionally, this type of research compares product features or competitive offerings in order to see what customers prefer. In the previous section, we reviewed the results of a research study that showed how much customers value relationships with companies with whom they do business. The idea for this study did not come out of thin air; for years I had made observations that suggested a powerful, emerging trend in our marketplace. Time and time again, I saw that customers' beliefs about products, services, or experiences pale next to feelings customers have for relationships with companies. The strongest brands are not about products or services, they are about relationships.

This is not the least bit surprising when you consider the question that introduced this section: Who do your customers love more, you or themselves? If they care more for themselves, wouldn't your customers be more interested in something that involves them—a relationship—than they would be interested in something that doesn't involve them, such as your product's features?

This is not to say that product features don't count. Of course they do. But most product categories in today's marketplace offer customers a number of good choices. Even if one product is truly better than the rest, customers often can't discern—or are unwilling

> **Make the brand about the customer AND you.**

to discern—fine differences between products. Customers are much more concerned about their own distinctiveness than they are concerned about the relative distinctness of competitive products.

The opportunity to create a truly powerful brand comes when you and your customer are able to wrap your product or service in a relationship. This amplifies the value and uniqueness of your product. Ensure that your brand isn't only about you. Make the brand about the customer *and* you.

The traditional concept of branding can't conceive of a brand that involves both a seller and a customer, because traditional branding is about promoting the reputation and awareness of a product among large groups of customers. These long-standing views of branding are much more concerned with a product's relationship with the entire marketplace. Instead, I find it much more powerful to think of a brand in terms of a relationship between your company or product and an *individual* customer.

A major theme of my book *Brand Harmony* is *"Your brand is not what you say you are, your brand is what your customer thinks you are."* There is often a wide gap between what companies claim in their marketing communications and what customers believe about them, and what really matters is what the customer thinks. For this reason, I equate a brand impression with a customer's beliefs about a company or product.

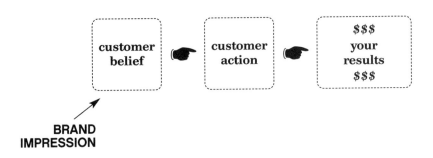

If a customer has beliefs about your company or your products that are compelling, motivating, and meaningful, that customer will be more likely to act in ways that improve your business results. As we have described above, the most compelling, motivating, and meaningful beliefs a customer can have about you involve the relationship she has with you. Strong brand impressions about relationships drive business results better than less compelling feelings for products, services, or experiences.

When I ask, "What brand impression do I want this customer to have of me?" I am not just asking what I want this customer to think of me, I am really asking, "What do I want my customer to think of our relationship?" If that feeling about our relationship is We, as opposed to Us & Them, my customer has created a particularly compelling brand impression in her mind.

Contrast the different actions customers are likely to take if they see their relationship as We instead of Us & Them: ⟶

Actions Customers are more likely to take...

	MORE LIKELY IN AN US & THEM RELATIONSHIP	MORE LIKELY IN WE RELATIONSHIP
You call when they are busy	They take a message	They take your call
You request a meeting	They commit reluctantly	They take the meeting without hesitation
You raise prices	They resist the increase and get competitive bids.	They are more likely to assume the increase is warranted
A delivery is late	They get upset	They forgive you
How they talk about you	Us & Them	WE
They meet someone who might need your services	They may refer you, perhaps with caution and reservation	They will refer you unequivocally and enthusiastically
They get a reference call asking if you are good	They will tell the bad with the good	They will eagerly serve as a reference
Budget time rolls around	They may take away money allocated to you if better things come up	They are more likely to increase their budget allocated to you
Their boss challenges them about why they are using you.	They cave in and get competititve bids	They tell their boss why they need you / they become your advocate
Projects move forward	They form teams that don't include your people	They include you on teams
They decide to create a new product	They send you (& your competitors) an RFP[1]	They involve you early on in the process
You spot opportunities for them	They resist your advice and assume you have a selfish motive	They take your advice and credit you for it

[1] Request for Proposal, i.e., corporate speak for "Let's see who will sell it to us the cheapest.

If a customer believes she is in a We relationship with you, she will be more likely to act in ways that are in your best interest.

- She will become a better customer.

- She will tell her friends how great you are.

- She will tell her boss that you are more than a supplier, and that she can't do her job as well without you.

- She will tell your competitors that she is not interested.

- She will not send out RFPs to multiple "vendors."

- She will never call you a "vendor."

Imagine if you call an incredibly busy client who is one of your We customers. He sees your number on caller ID, and his reaction is a feeling of solace and respite, of escape from his crazy day. He takes your call.

Wouldn't that be a profitable relationship?

We relationships are boundless; one We customer can be more valuable than many Us & Them customers. Smart companies will direct resources to transforming customer relationships from Us & Them to We. Time spent on establishing We relationships is a very profitable investment.

Who is the Customer?

My first job as a freshly-minted MBA in 1985 was with MTI Vacations, then one of the largest sellers of package vacations in the U.S. The secret to success in our business was persuading the airlines to sell us thousands of airplane seats at deeply discounted wholesale prices. It didn't take me long to realize that although we were a $50 million client of United Airlines, they were actually the customer.

My definition of a customer is simple: ***Anyone whose actions affect your business results***. The following chart, which we reviewed above, illustrates this:

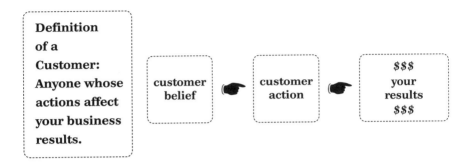

Don't be fooled by who is writing checks to whom. Ask a restaurateur trying to woo the top chef to come work for him. Ask any scrap metal dealer or used CD store owner whose business depends on being able to purchase an adequate supply of product. The seller is often the customer, because the seller often has the power to act in a way that affects the buyer's results.

A true We relationship is mutual. However, as the relationship is forming, it is common for one party to want the relationship more than the other. If you want to be in the relationship more than the other party does, you are the seller, even though you may technically be the buyer.

MARKETING TEACHES US THE WRONG THINGS ABOUT MARKETING

"WE'RE BECOMING EVEN MORE OF A SERVICE-BASED ECONOMY, AND 'WE' IS GOING TO BE INCREDIBLY IMPORTANT FOR SOMEONE WHO WANTS TO BE HERE TEN YEARS FROM NOW."—**DOUG DUCEY, CEO, Cold Stone Creamery**

This book will describe in detail what it takes to create and nurture We customer relationships. What will become increasingly clear is that the modern habit of being distant from your customer is a major impediment to We. Modern marketing techniques create great advertising but poor customer relationships. To create We relationships we must think beyond the traditional world of marketing.

If we can't turn to traditional marketing to provide a model for creating great customer relationships, where should we look?

Marketing Should Be Like Real Life

It's Friday evening, and Ted, a marketing executive, arrives home after a busy week at the office. He spends the evening with his family, and the kids eagerly share their stories from school. No one asks to leave the dinner table early, and there are moments when the family erupts in laughter as 6-year-old Molly describes a field trip to the zoo. On Saturday, Ted plays baseball with Jason, his 10-year-old, and teaches Molly to ride a bike. He and his wife, Sara, manage to leave early Saturday evening for a dinner date with friends, stealing an hour alone before arriving at the restaurant. The dinner is full of laughter, reminiscences, and warm interactions with these long-time friends. On Sunday, Ted and the family go to visit his parents' house, where the extended family has gathered for a barbeque. This, also, is a wonderful time filled with love, warmth, bonding, and conversation.

On Monday morning, Ted arrives at his office and sits down to discuss a marketing plan with his team. They discuss the best ways to communicate with their customers and decide to focus on radio advertising, billboards, and direct mail. They talk about "targeting" and "getting the word out." They discuss "messaging" and "breakthrough creative." Although his weekend has been filled with warm dialogue and genuine interactions, Ted shifts to a new mode of communication as he thinks through the marketing plan. He thinks monologue. He thinks "crafty and clever," so he can grab the attention of his audience. He imagines tens of thousands of people hearing his message. When he walked into the office he had checked Ted—husband, father, and friend—at the door and become just another marketing executive.

Ted knows how to create great relationships in his personal life. Why does he choose a completely different approach with his customers?

Of course, there are inherent differences between Ted's personal relationships and his customer relationships. He needs many more customers than he needs friends or family members. He can't possibly interact with each of his customers in the way he interacts with his family. But these differences are beside the point.

The more important issue to consider is this: What can he learn from the great relationships in his personal life to apply to his professional life? Instead of looking at traditional marketing tools as the ultimate in customer communication, should he instead look to the essence of human relationships as his model?

Relationships between human beings are among the most rewarding and most challenging aspects of our lives. When they go well, they're fulfilling. When they don't go well, things can be pretty miserable. Think about the times you or your friends are most unhappy—doesn't it usually have something to do with a relationship gone awry?

If we can understand what makes our personal relationships with other people succeed, we can learn important lessons about how to create relationships with customers. This doesn't mean that we are trying to be best friends with our customers. It just means that we can view the best relationships in our personal lives as a model for the relationships in our professional lives.

"I AND THOU"—SEEING AN OLD IDEA IN A NEW LIGHT

It is 6:00 a.m., still dark, as I drive into the parking lot at Chicago's Midway Airport while listening to an audiobook. Just before I turn the car off I hear the phrase, "Focus on engagement, not experience." I stop, rewind the tape, and listen again. It is one of those moments when I start to see everything differently. I am listening to a discussion of Martin Buber's landmark philosophical work from 1927, *I and Thou*.

Buber's premise in *I and Thou* is simple: We relate to people in two ways. The first is *I/It*. An *"It"* is a person with whom you have no personal connection. When you buy a quart of milk at the grocery store, you and the cashier are likely relating to each other as an "It." You give her cash; she gives you a receipt. You are interacting only to complete a transaction. To each of you, the other is interchangeable with any other cashier or customer. If you showed up at the same store tomorrow, it wouldn't matter to you if a different cashier were working. And, if the same cashier were working tomorrow, you probably wouldn't recognize one another. Often times *I/It* interactions like this are completely sufficient for the task at hand. We accomplish much each day through *I/It*—checking in for a flight, dialing up to check a credit card balance, paying for a car wash.

As I left the airport parking garage and walked into the terminal, I thought about Buber's second kind of relationship, *I/Thou*. This is more human, more rich, and more memorable than *I/It*. A person who is a *"Thou"* is not an object, but a person with whom you relate as distinct, unique human beings. The relationship is engaging. It is direct. It is meaningful. It has an impact on both of you.

When I approached the counter, the ticket agent looked me in the eye, and she asked me about my day. I wanted to change my seat. We discussed the available options and decided on one for me. "Let's keep you close to the front so you can get off quickly to make your connection in Washington," she said. I realized that she had related to me as a person, not just the next customer in line. She had *not* treated me as an interchangeable "It."

As I left the counter, I kept thinking about Buber's lesson. I had read *I and Thou* as an undergraduate, but, at that moment, I began to see how to apply his ideas to business. Buber recognizes that many of our interactions with people will be transactional "It" exchanges. But he also shows us the possibilities—the "what could be"—when we create something more than a distant connection with another human being. This "something more" is an *I/Thou* relationship. It is a relationship where the other person is not just an object in your thoughts or someone you use for personal gain, but a real person with whom you deeply engage.

My shoes were pretty scuffed up, so I walked to a shoe shine stand. The attendant, who introduced himself as Joe, had a lot of energy for 6:15 in the morning. He welcomed me into the seat, and we were immediately chatting about work and family. As Joe worked on my shoes, I noticed a newspaper lying on the next seat, opened to a page filled with ads for new blockbuster movies. I thought about the contrast between the movies and Joe. Although seeing a movie might be a great experience, it would be an *I/It* experience. Joe had moved beyond experience. He was engaging me as a "Thou," as a real person, not just as his next customer. At that moment, whose marketing was more effective—Joe's or the movie studio's?

Continuing on my way to the gate I grabbed a cup of coffee, sat down, opened my computer, and typed "From experience to engagement." Those were the first words I wrote for this book.

FROM EXPERIENCE TO ENGAGEMENT

There has been a great deal of talk in recent years about the necessity of creating outstanding experiences for customers. In 1999, Pine and Gilmore's *The Experience Economy* made the following important claim:

> Experiences are as distinct from services as services are from goods.[2]

How true, but the ante has been raised once more. Experiences are no longer enough. Many companies create compelling experiences for customers, telling their stories in ever more interesting ways. Experience alone is no longer a differentiator. Consider what happens every time one hotel chain creates a new enhancement to the guest experience, such as new amenities, upgraded bedding, or more exciting water slides at the pool. It doesn't take long for the competition to follow along, unimaginatively copy the innovation, and turn the unique experience into a commodity.

Although Buber never wrote about marketing, we can learn a valuable lesson from him about customer relationships. To create powerful, compelling, differentiating connections with customers, we have to move beyond creating experiences and telling stories, and focus on *engaging* with customers. Putting on a show for our cus-

---

[2]Joseph Pine and James Gilmore, *The Experience Economy*, (Boston: Harvard Business School Press, 1999), p. 2.

tomers is not enough. We must engage with customers and involve them in that show.

An experience can be staged with no personal connection to the audience, and it is not dependent on that audience. For example, a movie is a great experience, but it plays identically to an empty theater as it does to a full one. It is, essentially, monologue. Engagement, in contrast, depends on the specific players involved; it depends on both partners in the relationship. Engagement, through dialogue, inherently makes each encounter unique and personalizes each encounter.

Dr. Jay Ferraro, a psychologist with a practice focusing on Emotional Intelligence, described, in an interview I did with him, empathy as a key ingredient for engagement: "Empathy requires you to suspend judgment, opinion, and experience, and enter into the experience of another. Empathy makes engagement possible. If I can step out of my own experience and into another's, and demonstrate to that person that I feel what they feel, we will be able to resonate with each other emotionally."

Engagement is about human connection. It can be a deep, important conversation with a surgeon, or a simple, warm conversation with a flight attendant refilling your coffee. It is the difference between Buber's *I/It* and *I/Thou*, and it is the essence of the We relationship that is the subject of this book.

When you engage your customer, she does more than experience you and your product. She stands in relation to you. When the interaction is only one of experience, there may be entertainment, but there is also remoteness. I enjoy my experience at a professional baseball game, but there is an insuperable distance between the players on the field and me. I am an "It" to them, and they are "Its" to me, even though I know their stats and have read about their favorite foods and activities off the field. They entertain me, but they have no idea I am there. They would play no differently if I weren't there. We are not engaged.

However, when your customer's interaction with you moves beyond experience to engagement, the remoteness begins to evaporate. Engagement is a gateway to knowing each other. It may be unrealistic to expect professional baseball players to engage with fans (a fact that disappoints many 8-year-olds). But is it unrealistic to expect the experience you have at a local restaurant or a local retail store to rise to the level of engagement?

Engagement is never static. It flows like a dance. The movement of each person offers subtle guidance to the other about the shared direction in which they head. They are tuned into one another, playing off each other as the conversation moves in a shared direction. In the way a dancer subtly guides his partner with a nudge on the back, people who are engaged with each other lead one another in ways that feel like appropriate suggestions and welcome ideas.

A CUSTOMER MAY NOT NOTICE IF YOUR PRODUCT IS BETTER. **(But will notice if it's worse.)**

A CUSTOMER MAY NOT NOTICE IF YOUR SERVICE IS BETTER. **(But will notice if it's worse.)**

A CUSTOMER **WILL** NOTICE IF YOU ENGAGE WITH HER.

Where does engagement happen? As the next chapter explains, the forum for engagement is the *customer encounter*.

ENCOUNTERS: THE BUILDING BLOCKS OF WE RELATIONSHIPS

Transactions vs. Encounters

YOU & YOUR CUSTOMER COME INTO CONTACT.
WHAT HAPPENS?
IS IT A TRANSACTION OR AN ENCOUNTER?

A waiter takes your order, and five minutes later you want to ask him for something but you can't remember what he looks like. The process of ordering had been perfunctory and transactional. It is fleeting and has little meaning. You and the other person forget each other moments afterwards.

If you do happen to remember one another, it is not as individuals, but as members of categories of people. You think, "Was that my waiter? Did he have glasses?" He thinks, "I've got to check on table number five." Categories, not real people.

How often do we have these types of interactions in business? How often do we just interact with people for a minimal amount of time, with minimal effort and investment? Consider the last time your accounting department called a customer to collect on a bill, or the last customer service interaction you had with a customer. Was it, in essence, a very simple, clean, impersonal *transaction*? Or was it something more? Was it an *encounter?*

Transactions

Our lives are filled mostly with transactions, like the restaurant experience just described. Each day we buy things from stores and take the products home, but our relationships with these stores have not advanced a bit. Look at something next to you—a coaster on the table, a coffee cup, a book—can you remember the transaction, at some cash register, where you bought it? Can you remember the person who took your money and handed back the change? Unless they are negative, most transactions with businesses are void of meaning, unmemorable, and indistinguishable from other points of contact. They happen, they fulfill their basic function, and life goes on.

If you come in contact with your customer and your relationship doesn't change, or, worse, suffers damage, you have participated in a transaction. To build your relationship, you need something more than a transaction.

Encounters

My definition of an encounter: An encounter is a customer interaction that improves your relationship.

Our Definition

Encounters: interactions that improve your relationships

Transactions: interactions that often damage your relationship and, at best, have no effect on your relationship

Unlike a transaction, an encounter has a lasting, positive effect. It is more than a trading of goods, services, money, or information. It is a meeting with meaning. It is a collaborative interaction that brings its participants closer together.

Encounters require more energy than transactions, because transactions are often replays of past transactions. An encounter is a one-of-a-kind interaction that has never happened before. It draws on prior encounters for inspiration, but it is created for the here and now.

Encounters are the raw ingredients of a We relationship. They are inherently collaborative, giving the participants a feeling that they have done something together. Encounters are "moments of We" that build relationships.

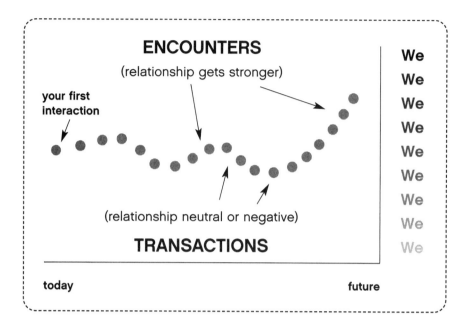

In a TRANSACTION...we are separate.
In an ENCOUNTER...we are in this together.

In a TRANSACTION...we trade words or goods back and forth.
In an ENCOUNTER...we engage with each other.

In a transaction...I am, to you, nothing but the role I play.
In an ENCOUNTER...I am me.

In a TRANSACTION...you are, to me, nothing but the role you play.
In an ENCOUNTER...you are you.

In a transaction...we use each other.
In an ENCOUNTER...we work with each other.

If encounters are what We relationships are made of, how do we create encounters?

AT THE CROSSROADS OF WE: THE THREE ELEMENTS OF A WE ENCOUNTER

There are three elements that save an interaction from the fate of becoming a meaningless transaction and allow it, instead, to become a relationship-building We encounter.

These three elements are: Engagement in the moment, conversation, and uniqueness.

> **1) Engagement in the Moment.** An encounter requires both parties to be present, attentive, and alert. An encounter is a rich moment in which you and your customer are fully engaged in the "now."

> **2) Conversation.** An encounter is much more than an exchange of monologues. It is dependent on fluid, interactive conversation.

> **3) Uniqueness.** An encounter is never scripted. It is always fresh. It is clear to the participants that the moment has never happened before. And, the people involved in an encounter are irreplaceable; they participate as special, unique human beings.

When these three elements are present, a mere interaction can become a lasting encounter, a building block of a We relationship. Let's explore these three elements of an encounter in depth.

ENCOUNTER ELEMENT #1: ENGAGEMENT IN THE MOMENT

3 ELEMENTS OF AN ENCOUNTER
one: engagment in the moment
two: conversation
three: uniqueness

The Encounter's Setting: A Moment with Presence

My first memory: I am less than two years old, and my grandmother and I are on an airplane. I am standing on the seat looking at her, and I see rays of sun through her hair from the window behind her. Years later, when I told her about this memory, she told me what we'd been doing, and I understood why this was my earliest memory. I'd been just learning to talk, and during the plane ride—probably less than an hour—she had been teaching me to say, "I love you, Daddy." She did a good job. When we landed in Chicago, I ran to my father shouting those words. She had been totally engaged in the moment with me for the entire plane ride. I couldn't help but be in the moment with her. And this memory stuck, from an age when I can remember nothing else. She died last year at age 96, and for the last 20 years of her life I watched her engage with my children whenever she saw them. They, too, have memories of those moments with her, and I'm sure they will carry those memories with them for the rest of their lives.

The stories of our lives are woven from moments. Vivid, special, and meaningful moments of presence create memories that shape who we are and how we see the world.

As a species, we are programmed to pay acute attention to the present. We have five highly developed senses and amazing cognitive abilities that enable us to interpret, in wonderful ways, what we perceive in a given moment. In contrast, we have absolutely no talent to predict the future with accuracy, and our sense of the past becomes fuzzy, distorted, biased, even lost, as time goes by. Using this natural ability to get the most out of the present moment is the first key to creating an encounter.

The Preparatory Mindset: It's Easy to Miss the Moment While You Prepare for Tomorrow

Despite our natural ability to be present in the moment, much of our training in life programs us to think more about what comes next rather than what we experience now. We spend each year in school preparing for the next year in school. Once we begin to work, we are always working hard for the next promotion. Then it all starts over as we teach our children how to live. We tell them, "If you don't start ballet lessons while you're young, you'll never have a chance!"

Planning for the future is, of course, an important part of creating a good life. However, aiming for the future can distract us from the moments along the way. Because we're always aiming, we're always waiting. Interim moments seem to have little value because we see them only as steppingstones to something yet to come. But then, when that time we have been waiting for finally arrives, it, too, becomes merely a way station to a new destination, and its present value pales in comparison.

We, of course, carry this preparatory mindset into our business lives. The purpose of a sales call is to prepare you to do business with a new customer. The waitress takes your order and looks at it only as a prelude to the act of delivering your food. The store clerk hands you a shirt in your size only as a mechanical step that prepares you to try it on. Transactions happen, but the opportunities for encounters are missed.

"Now" Has Value in Itself—Don't Miss It!

My band is in the recording studio, working on a new CD with our producer, Stuart Rosenberg, and our recording engineer, Mike Konopka. They've always helped us play our best. I'm adding a guitar track to a song, and I keep stopping, unsatisfied with how it sounds. It's slightly agitated; it seems forced. Stuart says, "You're playing all your notes a little early." He's right. I realize that I'm so anxious about the finished product that I'm not focused on my playing. I relax, fall into the tempo of the music, and my playing starts to flow. Mike smiles and says, "Sometimes people are in such a hurry to get where they're going that they miss the chance to enjoy what's happening right now."

> **Can't you tell when a sales person is more focused on the next step in his sales process than he is focused on the moment he is in with you?**

During a business-to-business sales process our preparatory mindset leads us to think of every sales call only as an interim step to something that will happen in the future. The purpose of the cold call is to get a meeting, the purpose of the first meeting is to get a second meeting, and the purpose of the second meeting is to be invited to make a proposal. Of course, these are natural steps in the sales process. However, if a salesperson only understands each step as a transaction on the way to the next step, he misses the opportunity to create an encounter. Customers can sense if a salesperson is too focused on getting to the next phase, as if he is on a hunt and he can only be satisfied with a successful conquest. On the other hand, a salesperson who engages a customer in the moment, in a great conversation, is much more likely to get, and, more significantly, to hold, the customer's attention. Having meaningful moments during the sales process improves the odds that the customer will make a purchase.

The same dynamic works in retail selling. Imagine a salesperson helping you pick out a jacket in a store. Is her job just to find a jacket for you to try on? What if she sees discussing available options with you as a meaningful moment, all in itself? An astute salesperson understands that looking through the racks with you is not just a mechanical process, but, in itself, something special. She will create a moment in which you can engage. After all, as you look at the coats on the rack, you are envisioning how you will look in them, who you will be with while you wear them, where you will be. She will figure out how to participate *with* you in that moment, not just find the jacket *for* you. She will, essentially, stand beside you, not across from you.

Moving a relationship ahead requires us to focus not only on the future of the relationship, but also on the moment that is happening right now. We must be engaged in the "now." We must be *present*.

Being Present

> After the death of his mentor the disciple was asked: "What was most important to your teacher?" The disciple thought and then replied: "Whatever he happened to be doing at the moment."[3]

I'm driving, and all of a sudden I realize that I've gone the last five minutes on autopilot. My mind has been elsewhere, thinking of work or friends or family. A very small part of me has been taking care of the driving.

How often do you put yourself on autopilot when you're talking with someone? We all have conversations where we really are *not* fully attentive. Our bodies are there, but our minds aren't.

When a newsletter on business networking recently crossed my desk, an article called "How To Extract Yourself From A Conversation" caught my eye. The article asked the question: How can you tell, at a business networking event, when the person you are talking to doesn't want to be in the conversation with you? Answer: When their eyes begin wandering around the room. When they shift their stance towards other people or the door. When the conversation lags. When they start answering in a monotone with words like, "interesting," "really," and "hmmmm."

My first reaction to reading this was that it was obvious; after all, an awkward, stiff conversation at a contrived business-networking event is not surprising. Then I thought about how frequently people attend to conversations from a distance in all types of business settings. We may be only partially present in a meeting that we don't want to attend, or not fully engaged in a conversation with some-

---

[3]Martin Buber, *Tales of the Hasidim*, Later Masters, "Most Important."

one who has stopped us in the hallway. Or maybe we're glancing at emails while we're on the phone with a customer. In all these cases, we are not really *in* the conversation. Our minds are occupied elsewhere.

To be present is not to be in another time or place, but to be here and now, engaged in this moment. It is to appreciate the current moment for its own merit, and to be aware of what it has to offer, devoting yourself to nothing but the encounter.

In a seminar recently, I asked a group of employees of Kimpton Hotels & Restaurants, a chain of 43 boutique-style hotels, what they thought it means to be present in the moment when they are with a customer. Carlo Stuart, the associate director of catering at Kimpton's Hotel Allegro said, "It means I'm loyal to my customer." I asked him to explain. "It's like tunnel vision," he continued, moving his hands in parallel from his face to where his customer would be. We usually think of "customer loyalty" as something our customers do for us. Carlo described it as something he does for his customers.

When I am totally present it seems to the other person that I am withholding nothing, that I am fully there with him. When I am not fully present, it is as if I have sent a personal functionary, a sliver of myself, to represent me. I am saying one thing, but thinking another. I have delegated the interaction to the smile on my face.

> **BE THERE NOW…** so you can be there in the future.

> **BE THERE NOW…** so your customer will want to be there with you in the future.

Various Strategies for Being Present

One of the greatest challenges to being present is the noise of modern life.

It can be difficult to shut out everything else in life and focus on the moment we are in right now. There are so many things to think about: all our friends and family, tasks we have to complete, phone calls we have to return, hundreds of emails, a stack of magazines to be read.

How do we ignore all these distractions? How do we shut them out, so we can focus on the moment we are in right now?

There is no single answer, but there are some guidelines. Each person may find different means for being present in the moment. My own ability to be present is very situational, depending on what I'm doing and what else is going on in my life. Sometimes it comes naturally, but there are many times when I am easily distracted and have to work at it. Following are a number of strategies I have learned over the years, all of which have worked for me and for other people I know at different times. Experiment. See which ones work best for you.

STRATEGIES FOR BEING PRESENT

- Pause before the moment
- Fall into the moment
- Be alert and notice the details
- Don't "pay" attention, invest it
- Observe the other person, & respond to what you observe
- Say "Yes" to the moment
- Don't be distracted by what you will get from the encounter

Each is described below.

STRATEGY: *Pause Before the Moment*

> I arrive at the restaurant for a meeting with only minutes to spare. I have been on a conference call in the car on the way, in heavy traffic, and my mind is not in the right place. But it is an important meeting that has taken weeks to set up with a prospective client. I really want it to go well.
>
> My first inclination is to jump out of the car and dash into the restaurant. But I stop myself. I don't move for a minute, thinking about the meeting. I envision the encounter I want to have. I imagine the ideal pace of the conversation. I take a breath. I create a line between the moment I am leaving and the moment I am about to enter. Now, I'm ready to go into the restaurant.

It is hard to enter an encounter cold. Prepare yourself for the moment, not by scripting it, but by envisioning it.

Preferably, you want more than a couple of minutes to get your mind in the right place. When I give speeches or run seminars, I am very conscious of the last hour before I hit the stage. I focus not only on what I will say, but on the tempo I want to set and what I hope the audience will take away from my presentation. I don't script the moment in advance, but I envision what the setting will be once the moment arrives. I don't know exactly what will be said or done, but I understand what kind of interactions will take place. This preparation makes it easier for me to engage in the moment.

Create a break. When calling a customer, don't shuffle through emails right up until he answers the phone. Use that moment to prepare for and think about the encounter that is about to happen. If you are in the lobby of a client's office waiting for a meeting to start, don't check your Blackberry. Use that time to get into the mode of the encounter. If you run into a customer on the street and he signals you to wait while he finishes a call on his cell phone, don't pick up your phone and check your messages. Use that moment to get ready for him.

TRY THIS>> **Before engaging in an interaction with a customer, stop and pause. Create a break, separating this encounter from what you've been doing. Envision the encounter. Think about the best pace for the encounter. Don't plan a script for it. Imagine its mood. Imagine what it will look like from the perspective of your customer.**

STRATEGY: *Fall into the Moment*

> I push through the turnstile at Wrigley Field, and the ticket taker hands my ticket back to me. I have to find Aisle 222, and the signs point me to the left. The game starts in 20 minutes, and a dense throng of people moves like logs flowing down a river through the stadium's corridor. I study the flow for a split second and spot an opening. I make my move into the mass of humanity and begin walking at exactly the same speed as everyone else. If I don't, I'll run into the person in front of me or be run over by the person in back of me. I don't try to change anyone's pace. I don't try to conduct the course of the whole line. I don't try to control anything. I just join.

You meet a customer in the middle of her action-packed day. She is in some sort of flow, doing things, thinking things. One of the best ways to engage in the moment with a customer is to see the moment she is in and fall into it with her. Adapt to her pace, mold yourself to her mood. Once you are in the moment with her, the encounter can go many places. But a good way to focus yourself is to fall into the moment your customer has already created.

This is especially true when you meet with a group of people in a company. As I write this, a colleague and I are flying to meet with three key executives in a client company. He and I have been talking about the client's current situation in order to envision the situation we will walk into when we arrive. That will help us be alert to the moment they are in when we meet them, so we can ease into it with them.

Recognize that the moment is already happening, with or without you. Witness it, sense it, feel it. You are about to join a moment already in progress. Pay attention to what is going on before you jump in. You may only have a second to observe, but, even in that short instant, you can be alert to what is happening around you.

> ┌──────────────┐
> │ **TRY THIS>>** │ **Approach a group of friends or colleagues who are**
> └──────────────┘ **in the middle of a conversation. Before speaking,**
> **notice the pace of the conversation, the dynamics of their interaction.**
> **See it like a river current. If you were to ease into its stream, how**
> **would you do it? Now, join the flow of this moment already in progress.**

STRATEGY: *Be Alert and Notice the Details*

"USE YOUR SENSES FULLY. BE WHERE YOU ARE. LOOK AROUND. JUST LOOK, DON'T INTERPRET. SEE THE LIGHT, SHAPES, COLORS, TEXTURES. BE AWARE OF THE SILENT PRESENCE OF EACH THING… LISTEN TO THE SOUNDS; DON'T JUDGE THEM…MOVE DEEPLY INTO THE NOW."—ECKHARD TOLLE, *The Power of Now*

After you enter the moment, notice what is going on. Let the moment continue to speak to you. Use your senses to become more deeply engaged in the moment.

There are always beautiful details to notice. Although it may not be apparent at first, there is a beauty in every encounter, in every moment, which may not be clearly visible at first. But if you listen to that moment and allow it to reveal itself, it will disclose what makes it special and noticeable.

Zoom in. Notice the small details that make up the moment. Don't worry just yet about how they fit in with the big picture. That will come. For now, just notice the details.

Now, pull your lens back and notice small groups of details with similar characteristics. Then, zoom back further, and focus for a moment on the big picture. Do you notice any themes or common characteristics among the details, or interesting ways in which they complement each other?

Let the details, and the interplay between different details, draw you into the moment. You may find that the details are "hooks" that engage your focus and shield you from distractions outside of this moment.

TRY THIS>> Put on headphones in a dimly lit room, and listen to some of your favorite music—something you have heard many times. Listen to the music as a whole, and then pay attention to the individual instruments one at a time. Notice what each of them is doing. Notice the character and nuance of each instrument, the details within the details. Picture the human behind the playing, what it feels like to be playing that instrument or singing that vocal part. Now, zoom out from the details and see how different parts fit together. Are you hearing details you have never heard before in this music? Are you engaged in the music in a new way?

STRATEGY: Don't "Pay" Attention, Invest It

> I am in first grade. The teacher asks the class to pay attention. I notice the word "pay." I saw my mom pay at the grocery store. She took money from her purse and gave it to the person at the cash register. I saw my father take money from his wallet and pay at the gas station. Now it is my turn to pay something. To whom do I pay it?

In English we use the term "paying attention." Why do we have to "pay" it? Does that mean that our attention is something valuable that we don't want to part with, like money? Do we look at this payment as a loss of something? Are we giving up something when we pay attention?

In Hebrew, the idiom for paying attention is "sim lev," or, literally, "putting heart" into something. It doesn't cost me anything to put my heart into something; it isn't a payment at all. It is an investment. I know I'll get much back in return, something that will enrich me.

To put my heart into something is to put my whole self into it. The heart represents my entire ticking being, not just a representation of me, but the actual living process of me. To pay attention is to fully invest in this moment. You don't give up anything when you pay attention. In fact, paying attention has a high return on investment.

> **TRY THIS>>** As you pay attention to things today, be aware of what that attention returns to you. Focus not on what you give when you pay attention, but on what you receive.

STRATEGY: *Observe the Other Person, and Respond to What You Observe*

> Roslyn Alexander is an award-winning actress who has played stages in Chicago and New York for decades. She is also my aunt. Roz relates her experiences on the stage, when she has to engage in the moment with another actor: "React off the other person. As they move, you move. It's like dancing. Be very aware of what they are doing and respond to it. Look for their cues. If they look disbelieving, play off it. If they seem in awe, enjoy it. Go with them. Observe the details."

People are interesting. Even boring people are interesting, relative to so many other things we can think about. Later in this book, we will talk much about how the details of a person's character make them unique and special. For now, consider how noticing these details can be an effective way to engage you in the moment with that person.

If you notice the interesting features, the personality quirks, the idiosyncratic movements, or even the vocal inflections of a person you meet, you can latch onto those characteristics as a way to become present and engaged in the moment.

> **TRY THIS>>** In your personal conversations today, notice everything you can about the person with whom you are speaking. Notice how they look, what they say, how they say it. Understand how they are feeling, based on how they sit or stand, how they move, what they say. Let the things you notice pull you into the moment with each person.

Then, do the same thing in your next conversations with customers. Notice everything you can about customers as you speak with them.

Let the things you perceive about each customer guide you into the encounter.

STRATEGY: Say "Yes" to the Moment

Have you ever seen actors improvise a scene on stage? How do they do it? How do they walk out in front of a crowd without a script and create a captivating scene?

> I dial my client's number for a scheduled conference call. I am planning to speak with two people from this company to review market research results from the field. The results are definitive and powerful. I am very eager for this call, because I believe that the results I have to report provide important direction for our project. However, once the call starts, it becomes clear that my clients have a different agenda for this conversation. They have just come from a meeting with top management who want us to prepare a project update presentation for them in two weeks. My clients are not interested in digging deep into the research results—as I am. Instead, all they want to discuss is this imminent presentation to top management.
>
> I am very frustrated by this detour. I want to explore the deep nuances of the research data and discover exciting treasures in the information. In contrast, all they want to talk about is creating a "sound bite" for management people with "short attention spans." That seems like a pretty easy thing to do, so I impatiently say, "We can do that, it should be easy. Now, let's dig into the research data." But they return again to their agenda, and I again try to steer us back to the discussion of the research. This is not a good conversation.

I was wrong. I should have accepted the situation and changed my course. They needed to dwell on this issue for a bit longer, and they wanted to feel that I understood how important it was to them. Had I given them a little more time to discuss the issue and shown more empathy for it, we would have been able to move quickly on to the research I wanted to discuss. Ultimately, I would have had a better chance of having the discussion I wanted if I would have taken the route they presented me. I should have said "Yes" to the moment they were in. I should have engaged in their moment.

Actors engaged in stage improvisation use a technique called "Yes, and" to create an extemporaneous scene. The idea behind "Yes, and" is simple: No matter what one of your fellow actors says or does, you do not resist. If the two of us are improvising a scene set in a convenience store, and all of a sudden you act startled and say, "A tyrannosaurus rex is about to come into the store!" I do not say, "No, it isn't." Instead, I say, "And it's got a baby pterodactyl in its jaws!" Whatever you say, I say "Yes," and then I say "and..." to move our conversation forward.

We often find ourselves in situations that aren't going the way we want them to. The immediate reaction we have in these situations is to resist the moment, and focus on how much we don't like what's going on. A number of years ago I received some good advice on dealing with these situations from a yoga instructor, Jai Luster. At the time, Jai was a hedge fund executive by day teaching yoga for the sheer love of it in his off-hours. He has since retired from the financial world to focus on yoga full time. Jai says that the first challenge is to recognize that you are resisting the situation. He describes this as "confronting the 'I don't want to.'" He explains: "If I am in a conversation that I don't want to be in, the first thing I have to do is notice that I'm resisting. This may seem simple, but it can be tricky. If I am aware enough to spot my resistance, I'm halfway there, because then I will find it easier to accept the situation. It's a funny thing—the resistance is tougher if you don't realize you're doing it."

If you resist the moment, it will definitely be a transaction. If you confront the "I don't want to" you may be able to make it into an encounter. Say "Yes" to whatever is happening. Don't follow your own script. It will then be much easier to get to where you want to be.

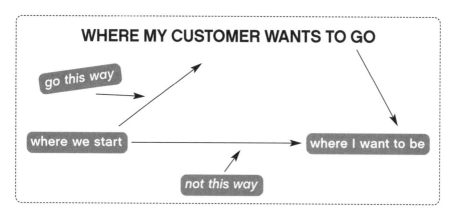

TRY THIS>> As you talk with friends, family members, and customers over the next few days, notice the path they want to take in the conversation. Be aware, and be patient. Without losing sight of what you would like to have happen in the conversation, accompany the other person in the direction they would like to go. Then, as the dialogue unfolds, look for sensible, genuine ways to bring the conversation toward the direction you want to go.

Be willing to navigate a course that seems most comfortable for the person with whom you are speaking. Remember, sometimes the clearest path to the goal in a conversation with someone may look like a detour to you, but a straight line to them.

STRATEGY: Don't Be Distracted By What You Will Get From the Encounter

> One day a man was watching a tightrope walker with rapt attention. His friends asked why he was so absorbed in the spectacle. "This man is risking his life, and I cannot say why. But I am quite sure that while he is walking the rope, he is not thinking of the fact that he is earning a hundred gulden by what he is doing, for if he did, he would fall."[4]

It is good to be results oriented. But too much focus on the outcome of the encounter can take your focus off the encounter itself. You

---

[4]Martin Buber, *Tales of the Hasidim*, Early Masters, "The Rope Dancer."

need to have your "eye on the prize," but, as in the case of the tightrope walker, concentrating on the desired result could mean a misstep.

Yes, you are in relationships with customers for profit. It is perfectly natural—and necessary—to want to gain benefit from a customer relationship, so it is also natural to think about those benefits during an encounter. To stay in the moment, however, try to avoid anxiety over possible gains. For example, during a sales call I actively search for a good outcome, but I try to suspend any thoughts or fears about whether I will be able to close the deal. I find that the less I focus on what I will get from the sales process, and the more I focus on creating a great encounter, the more likely it is that the other person will be willing to do business with me. If I have anxiety about the outcome, they can see it, and that is what they focus on.

Another way to avoid anxiety about the outcome is to remember that you, as well as the customer, have a choice about whether you will come to an agreement. Always remind yourself that you are scrutinizing the customer while he is scrutinizing you, and you have a say about whether you move forward together with the relationship. You are never at the mercy of any customer; you must believe that you have control over what happens. Recognizing this will reduce anxiety and distractions about the outcome of any encounter.

Take your eyes *off* the prize for a minute. Do not grasp for the outcome. Don't be distracted by what you will get from the encounter, or you will be less likely to achieve it. Focus on making the present encounter as good as it can be. Trust that great encounters lead to great outcomes. This is not easy, but it is important.

TRY THIS>> **In conversations with customers, practice having your goal be a good encounter. Even if it is difficult, tell yourself that other outcomes are secondary. Don't worry that your customer may decide not to buy, or may decide something else that affects you adversely. Focus on having a great encounter.**

These strategies, and others that you may devise for yourself, can help you be present in any moment to create an encounter. In the next section, we will explore strategies for inviting your customer into the moment with you.

Invite Your Customer into the Moment

Imagine yourself the host of a Japanese tea ceremony. When your guests arrive they do not go directly into your home. According to tradition, you greet them outside and sprinkle water across their path in order to signify a break with the outside world and help them enter the world of the tea-house. This transition helps them leave the distractions of life outside, so that they can enter your tea ceremony and enjoy it with their full presence.

Although you may be fully present and focused on turning this interaction into an encounter, your customer may not feel the same. He may be lost in the distractions of his own day, or maybe he hasn't yet realized an interest in having an encounter with you. Perhaps you are trying to sell something to a group of Blackberry-toting, over-stressed executives who are squeezing you into a day of back-to-back meetings. Or, you are working at the front desk of a hotel, and your customer is a tired, haggard business traveler who has just endured a delayed flight from home and a traffic jam during the cab ride from the airport. Whatever the situation, the encounter depends on your success in inviting your customer into the moment. Otherwise, you will be in the moment alone, and your conversation will resonate with the sound of one hand clapping.

NOTICE>> Think about interactions you've had, as a customer, over the last week. Did companies invite you into the moment with them, or were there obstacles to engaging with them?

┌─────────────────────────────────┐
│ **HOW DO YOU COMPARE>>**   │ Now, think of what it is like to be
└─────────────────────────────────┘ your customer. Does your organization invite customers into the moment? Do you make it easy for customers to engage with you?

Think about what it would take for you to do a better job of inviting
customers into the moment. What are the obstacles? Where are you
falling short?

Your Presence Makes Invitation Possible

The most obvious thing to remember at this point is that you are
inviting your customer to *join you* in the moment. You are not ushering him into an empty space, like a doorman ushering someone into
the back of a cab. You are inviting your customer into a space in
which *you* are already present and engaged.

Your presence and engagement in the moment communicate
that there is a moment happening that can be entered. In a We
encounter, you welcome your customer into the moment the way the
host of the tea ceremony welcomes his guests. You offer a transition
from the moment in which he has been immersed, to the one that
you have prepared for him.

> Alan Malmed, M.D., a radiologist in the Chicago area, tells
> me during an interview: "This is the way many people meet
> me: They are waiting in a cold room at the hospital for some
> doctor to show up and extract tissue from their body for a
> biopsy. They are frightened for their health and scared of
> the procedure. They are expecting a cold, unconcerned
> doctor. As I come into the room and the technician intro-
> duces me, I can see worry on the patient's face. After saying,
> 'Hello,' the next thing I do is sit down. This communicates
> that I will take my time with them. I am not in a rush."

Dr. Malmed sits down as a way to invite his customer into the
moment. This shows his patient that he is present, that he is there
with the patient, not just there to do something *to* the patient.

In some cases, a moment of eye contact can communicate your
presence in the moment. A conspicuous pause also signals your

> **Dr. Malmed shows the patient that he is there WITH him, not just there to do something TO him.**

presence, whether it is an extra second taken during a handshake, or an obvious break in your activity at the first moment of interaction.

Your alertness also communicates your presence. As we described earlier, your alertness brings you into a moment; heightened senses focus you on your immediate surroundings and keep distractions at bay. That same alertness is, I am convinced, clear and obvious to another person. We can't help but wear our alertness as a bright badge, visible to everyone who sees us. If you are visibly in tune with the moment, you will signal your presence to another, welcoming him into the moment.

> **TRY THIS>>** In your next interaction with a friend or customer, focus on making your own presence and attention visible to the other person. Be genuine, don't force it, or it won't seem like you are really present. Just *be* present, and show it.

Listening Is Inviting

Simply by letting the other person speak first, you open a lit pathway through which that person can join you in the moment.

Later we will discuss, in depth, the importance of dialogue and conversation in the creation of an encounter. For now, let us focus on how conversation creates an inviting moment for your customer. Your focus on them communicates your attention and acts as a beacon to welcome them in. Listen. Let them speak.

Dr. Jay Ferraro, who was introduced in Chapter 1, recommends that we "listen contextually." He says that, "in order to resonate with another person, it helps to speak at their pace and tone, and even to integrate their language into the conversation." Dr. Ferraro also cautions us to suspend judgment as we hear a customer speak. "Our natural inclination is to offer fixes and solutions, but this is an obstacle to empathy. It can cause the other person to put up a wall of defense."

Stuart Rosenberg, my music producer mentioned above, is a Chicago-area musician, writer, and producer. He describes how he uses listening to engage a potential customer in a discussion about music for their wedding. "I like to ask surprising questions that go beyond the matter at hand. 'What are the buttons on your radio pre-set to? Do you remember listening to your parent's records as a kid?' They are not expecting those questions, but they love answering them. As I listen to their answers, they get involved in the conversation, and I get interesting ideas about how to create music for their celebration."

People want to be heard. Be alert for things the other says that genuinely interest you, and allow your interest to be visible. Jai Luster, the retired hedge fund manager turned yoga entrepreneur we met before, describes how listening engages someone: "When you listen, people know you are listening. When they are heard they feel like they exist."

And, of course, be sure that your attention is genuine. You can't engage another person if you're faking it. The only enthusiasm that is infectious is that which is real.

NOTICE>> Notice how much easier it is for you to engage with people when they listen to you.

TRY THIS>> If someone does not seem fully ready to engage with you, give them plenty of space to talk. **Listen actively. Show you are listening. Does your listening help them engage?**

She Has Reasons Not to Join You

Customers have many reasons not to accept your invitation to join you in the moment. Their lives, like yours, are cluttered and filled with noise. People only have so much time for engaging encounters, so it is desirable, necessary even, for all of us to keep many of our daily interactions at the level of mere transactions.

It is natural for all of us to put up shields as others try to invite us into moments. I deflect a salesperson's offer of help with "I'm just looking." A fundraiser from a theater where I have a subscription series calls on the phone and I dismiss his attempts to draw me into a conversation about a special fund drive. We do this as customers, and we confront it from our customers. We must earn the right to have a customer join us in the moment.

Recently, I was in San Francisco on a business trip. Still on Chicago time, I woke up at 5:30 a.m. with this book on my mind. By 6:15, I was sitting in a Starbucks writing this section about how to invite your customer into the moment. I happened to overhear a Starbucks employee talking with a customer about this same topic. "Everybody is so ready to say 'no,' and I love the challenge of making them say 'yes.'" After they finished their conversation, I approached the employee, whose name is Rob Lemen, manager of this Starbucks location. "I couldn't help but hear what you said, and I think it's related to something I was just writing about. Would you mind telling me the story?"

"No problem," Rob answered. "When people come in here, they're programmed to say 'No.' They've just run the gauntlet of people on the street asking them for money or trying to hand them flyers, and they've just had to say 'No' a lot of times. What's funny is that when I ask people if they want me to leave room for cream in their coffee, 80 percent of the people who actually do want cream automatically say 'No.' And then, after a pause, they say 'Oh, wait a second. Yeah.' I can see when people come in like this. It's like they've got blinders on, with this really focused look on their faces. So I go over the top as far as trying to be welcoming and inviting."

Rob's personal approach is to use humor to break the ice with customers and engage with them as they wait in line. It turns out that his Starbucks is the busiest in San Francisco. "Sometimes when it's busy, I'll go down the line and take people's drink orders and also ask them if they want food. If they say 'No,' I break through that...I'm not trying necessarily to turn them around...but I'll joke around with people and say 'Hey, you know breakfast is the most important meal of the day. Are you taking care of yourself? Does your mother know you're not eating breakfast?' Stuff like that. Just to get a laugh and make them feel, again, more welcomed and just joke around with them and develop that rapport to make them feel comfortable." While Rob uses humor, your personal approach to inviting a customer to engage with you may be different. The particular approach is not critical. What matters is recognizing when your customer has obstacles to engaging with you, and doing whatever you can to make it easier for the customer to enter the moment with you.

Although Doug Stevenson grew up in the shadows of Chicago's Wrigley Field, it was theater, not baseball, that caught his imagination as a teenager. After playing stages in Los Angeles for years, Doug developed a very successful career as a public speaker, employing his acting skills to connect with his audiences. Doug's passion lies in using story as a way to engage audiences in public speaking and customers in a sales process. Doug offers some interesting advice for a situation where a customer resists engaging in the moment with you as you're trying to make a sale. "Sometimes a prospect will say 'Okay, give me your pitch. You know, do your thing. I don't have a lot of time today, so go ahead.' He isn't that interested in being there with me, and the easy thing for him to do is just have me do my salespitch. Well, if I use a story to make the pitch, it causes them to participate and listen at a deeper level. The fascinating thing about story is that if I tell someone a story, halfway through my story they are starting to prepare their story in response to my story."

As we will see below, when you tell your story to a customer you must be careful to avoid creating a monologue that doesn't engage your customer. However, if you heed this caution, use of story can be a great way to invite a customer into the moment. Doug explains: "A story is a great way to get someone to engage…hearing a good story causes people, in an almost Pavlovian way, to have to tell their own story." Doug explains why people have a harder time engaging with a sales pitch that just explains features and benefits. "An explanation is basically a logical discussion of facts that goes directly into our left brain. And the left brain doesn't do any interpreting; it just kind of files things away. But story takes you out of logic and into imagery and emotion. Story goes into the more creative and interpretive right brain. It's using imagination rather than the logic of the current situation."

She May Not Realize She is Not Joining You in the Moment

Often a customer isn't consciously aware that she is avoiding joining you in the moment. In addition to leading a large congregation in Glenview, Illinois, Rabbi Karyn Kedar is the author of three books, *God Whispers, Dance of the Dolphin*, and *Bridge to Forgiveness*. She describes a situation that happens frequently in her counseling sessions with members of her congregation. A congregant will come to see her for help, at a time of great crisis in his or her personal life. Going into the session, Rabbi Kedar knows enough about the situation to expect great emotion and, most likely, tears. However, the person frequently begins the session speaking dispassionately, telling Rabbi Kedar about the situation, describing various aspects, and, importantly, discussing how other people feel about the situation. "My mother's illness is really troubling my brother." "I don't know how my father will cope once she is gone." The congregant tells her about the situation, but at a distance from her true feelings. Rabbi Kedar calls this "reporting." This distance prevents the congregant from being in a moment that, in this case, could be very emotional and healing.

Rabbi Kedar's first challenge in these situations is clear. She has to bring the customer into the moment in a way that is real, and not reported from a distance. Then, healing becomes possible.

"Aboutism"

The gestalt psychologists have a term for what Rabbi Kedar calls reporting. They call it "aboutism." Talking *about* something is a safe thing to do. I can tell you *about* my mother's illness and, by doing it at a distance, I can shield myself from really feeling the pain of the situation. Or, on a business level, if I tell you *about* my business, it is possible for me to report on the situation without ever letting you—or me—near it.

Businesspeople often fall into the "about" trap. Consider how people in a company talk about their customers, using broad demographic categories to describe who they are ("Hip thirty-something female executives") or theoretical attitudes to describe what the customers want. ("Our customers relish a feeling of exclusivity, as if they have learned a privileged code that others have yet to crack.") This all sounds good, but does it help us really know what would make an individual customer love the company? Think of an executive describing his mission statement: "We are the #1 provider of fermented widgets serving the natural gas industry, exceeding our customers' expectations and striving for excellence and community service in everything we do." Can you imagine someone actually talking like that in their personal life? Of course not!

Talking about a business gives one a false sense of comfort, while shielding him from really feeling his situation.

I'm in my car and my cell phone rings. It's a client who tends to call me a lot, especially after meetings with his fellow senior executives. He recaps the problems of the company, "Sales volume from large customers is down, deliveries are late, and the VP of operations doesn't seem to understand his role in the situation … " I'm struck by how factually and dispassionately my client speaks; it's as if he is a Wall Street analyst talking about someone else's company. He is a key executive and part owner of the company, with everything to lose. Where is the passion? I recognize the disconnect between his reporting about his situation and his deeper feelings. I know he's avoiding facing the real issues, because they are uncomfortable. But I can't help him unless he engages in a real conversation with me.

"Bill," I ask him, "if you call me a year from today, on the way home from next September's meeting, what will we be talking about?"

Silence for a moment.

"Steve, if we don't change, I don't know if there will be a meeting next September."

Now, we can make some progress.

Helping Your Customer Avoid "Aboutism"— STRATEGY #1: Bring the Future Forward

The conversation with Bill, above, illustrates one of my favorite ways to help a customer stop reporting about a situation and engage deeply in the present moment—bring the future forward.

It is ironic, but undeniably true: It's easier to be in the moment thinking about the future than it is when thinking about today. Today is filled with distractions, phone calls to make, appointments to keep, situations to deal with. So, when we think about today it's sometimes hard to really *be here*. But, we can often see a future day more clearly, because it is relatively uncluttered. By visualizing a future time, the present becomes more clear.

Last week a client and I were discussing my proposal to create an employee marketing program. We had just finished developing a brand strategy for his company, and we were discussing how important it would be to ensure that employees throughout the company completely understood and believed in the brand strategy. Instead of having an intellectual, rational conversation *about* the merits of this initiative, I initiated a discussion in which we imagined different interactions between his employees and customers, at a point in the future. I asked him to imagine it was a year from now. Together, we formulated scenarios, one in which an employee did not live out the brand strategy, and another where he was totally enrolled in the strategy. As we described realistic, understandable situations involving individual employees and individual customers in the future, I could feel the conversation kick into a different gear. This imagining of real future moments helped us to create a shared understanding, in which we both saw clear visions of the benefits of this initiative. We had stopped talking *about* the initiative and, instead, we both *felt* the initiative. The acceptance of my proposal—which I believed to be 100 percent in his best interest—became a *fait accompli*.

> **We had stopped talking about the initiative and instead, we both felt the initiative.**

Bringing the future forward can work in many settings. Earlier, I used the example of a sales clerk in a clothing store turning the process of finding a jacket into a meaningful moment. She could bring the future forward by asking "What kind of places will you be wearing this jacket?" or "Think of yourself being there, wearing each jacket. Which one feels better?"

Or, imagine yourself as a residential real estate agent, working with clients who were being overly analytical about two different houses, talking "about" all the relative merits of each, but finding themselves unable to make a decision. You might say, "Stop for a minute and think about Thanksgiving dinner. First in one house, and then in the other. Who is there, what are you doing, what are you eating? Imagine dinner is over, and you and your guests sit down in the living room to talk. Which house is more comfortable for that occasion?" Bringing a future moment into the present is a great way to help a customer live in that present moment. Thoughts of the future are, ironically, safe in most cases. We can easily imagine how things will be at a later date, and this makes it easier for us to feel the present moment.

Stuart Rosenberg describes an interesting way to bring a future moment into the present to create a rich conversation with a customer. When Stuart has been contracted to provide music for a wedding, a common scenario is a meeting with a frantic mother-of-the-bride three weeks before the big day. The pressure of the planning is weighing hard on mom, and it's often difficult to get her to focus on a discussion of the music. "Since I have been to hundreds of weddings, I know what kind of magic this mother is going to feel three weeks from now at the reception, in that first hour after her daughter has been married. But she is so distracted by what is happening right now, she can't feel that magic. If I can get us talking about the reception, and can take a spark from that future time and bring it back into the conversation we want to have right now, it will be much easier for her to talk about the music with me. She will see our conversation as part of that magic, and not just see it as another thing to check off her list."

Here are a few more examples I have used in my consulting business to bring the future forward into the present moment to engage a customer:

> "Imagine it's December 31st of next year, and you are just about to leave the office to go to a New Year's Eve party. You and your colleagues are celebrating a great year, pointing to numbers on reports that illustrate how successful you were. What are you looking at on those reports?"

> "If we were talking about this project a year from now, what would make us think it has been really successful?"

> "Imagine two years from now I am sitting in a booth in a restaurant and I overhear some people talking about your company. I realize they are customers. What would they be saying about you?"

> "Imagine a year from now I am standing in line to buy a cup of coffee and I hear two people in front of me talking. They are your employees. What would they be saying about the company?"

Helping Your Customer Avoid "Aboutism"— STRATEGY #2: Use Someone Else's Words

In addition to bringing the future forward into the present moment, the final two examples above also illustrate another strategy that I have found to be effective to help a person stop reporting about a situation and engage fully in the moment. This strategy is to have them speak in someone else's words.

For example, when helping a company better define their identity and brand essence, I often ask my clients to describe their value to the world not in their own words, but in the words of their customers. "Don't tell me what you think," I ask, "imagine right now, at this very minute, a customer is telling a friend or colleague about how much she loves doing business with you. What would she be saying?"

People often fall into the "aboutism" trap because they have heard themselves tell the same stories so many times that they become desensitized to them. They switch to "autopilot" as they talk about something, relating thoughts that have become so familiar to themselves that they seem routine.

By encouraging your customer to describe a situation in someone else's words, he will be forced to think beyond the automatic explanations he is used to giving. He will have a fresh perspective that can help him go beyond reporting about a situation to actually feeling it. Then he will engage with you, and you can create a meaningful encounter.

You can use this concept in many ways. Depending on your particular type of customer encounter, you may ask a customer to describe a situation in the words of his friends, employees, colleagues, bosses, bankers, or competitors, to name just a few possibilities.

Helping Your Customer Avoid "Aboutism"— STRATEGY #3: Empathy and Engagement

A person who is reporting "about" something is not engaged with the other person; he is actually not even engaged with himself. He is telling a story from a distance. Earlier, we read Dr. Jay Ferraro's description of how empathy leads to engagement. Dr. Ferraro explains the difference between acknowledgment and validation to describe how your empathy can help your customer move beyond "aboutism". "Acknowledgment is just showing the person that I understand the content of what he says. 'I hear that you're really concerned about your market share.' Or, 'So, your employees are not being very effective in the use of your new sales program.'" Validation goes further. It shows that I not only understand the content of what the other person is saying, I understand what the situation means to that person. 'So, I can really hear that you're concerned that sales are down and your people are not using your new sales program. I'll bet you're really frustrated by that, and it must be causing you a lot of turmoil.' This is empathy, and it can help the conversation move from 'aboutism' to engagement. Now I'm in relationship mode with that person. If I'm resonating with what's going on inside of this person's soul, their gut, their heart, their mind, then I am engaged with them. And that is the basis of relationship." What is fascinating about Dr. Ferraro's advice is that he is recommending that we engage in our customer's situation, even if the customer is not engaged in it, but only reporting about it. Don't let your customer's "aboutism" trap you; if you can avoid "aboutism" in the conversation, you will help your customer break away from it.

Then you can invite your customer into the moment for a relationship-building encounter.

> **TRY THIS>>** If you notice someone "reporting" about a situation that you want them to feel more closely, try the three techniques we have just discussed:

● Bring the future forward by discussing a point in the future that is free from the constraints and distractions of today.

● Encourage them to describe a situation in someone else's words.

● Focus on being empathetic. Go beyond acknowledging the other person's situation. Validate it.

Media: Obstacles to Invitation and Engagement

"BEFORE THE IMMEDIACY OF THE RELATIONSHIP, EVERYTHING MEDIATE BECOMES NEGLIGIBLE." —MARTIN BUBER, *I AND THOU*

"EVERY MEANS IS AN OBSTACLE. ONLY WHEN EVERY MEANS HAS COLLAPSED DOES THE MEETING COME ABOUT...IN FACE OF THE DIRECTNESS OF THE RELATION EVERYTHING INDIRECT BECOMES IRRELEVANT."—MARTIN BUBER, *I AND THOU*

When you go into a convenience store to buy something, you often pass your money to a person who sits in a small, enclosed area behind bulletproof glass, with a small, metal half-pipe passageway under the glass. Imagine trying to have a frictionless, fluid conversation with that person. The barrier would make it difficult.

Now think of this bulletproof glass as a metaphor for the barriers between you and your customers. What portion of the conversations that you have with customers are indirect and mediated, whether it be by an email, a letter, or a brochure?

Or…are they immediate?

The word "immediate" means "nearest in time, space, or relationship … affecting something directly without anything intervening." An interaction is mediated anytime there is something between you and your customer. It is much more difficult to be in a moment with your customer and create an encounter when there are obstacles between you. It is possible, as with a great phone conversation, but it is always more difficult than in a direct, immediate encounter.

As we discussed earlier, there are many modern marketing technologies that enable companies to talk directly with their customers. Most discussions about marketing, however, reflexively assume a use of third-party media to communicate a story. Advertisements, mailings, brochures, and websites are traditionally thought of as the primary carriers of marketing messages. What do all of these have in common? They are stuck between the seller and the customer. They do not involve direct contact between the two parties.

Of course, many of these media are necessary. After all, we can't always be present, in person, with our customers. However, these mediated messages should not be seen as the primary means of marketing communication, but as "necessary evils" that supplement and complement the more critical and vital direct encounters we have with our customers. If you can't be there in person with your customer, it may be necessary to delegate communication to a magazine, a web site, or a distributor. But, when possible, get the media out of the way and meet your customer directly.

A direct, *immediate* encounter makes possible frictionless interaction with your customer. A *mediated* contact, with a brochure or ad, can never communicate as well—or as interactively—as an immediate encounter.

A friend challenged me on this point, giving an example where an indirect, mediated communication to a customer can be more effective than direct communication with the customer. The example

> See media in marketing not as the primary means of communication, but as necessary evils.

he gave is word of mouth marketing; after all, isn't it more effective when a customer raves about you than when you rave about yourself? No doubt. But notice that the origin, the motivating event, of any third party recommendation is a direct, unmediated encounter. For example, if someone recommends a restaurant or an accountant to me, their enthusiastic opinion will be based on direct, immediate encounters, not on a brochure, ad, or website.

As noted earlier, marketing traditions and tools developed over recent decades have put distance between sellers and their customers. Mass marketing vehicles, database technologies, customer relationship management programs that allow companies to delegate the management of customer relationships to a computer—all these things, and many others, have made it possible to view customers as distant objects. Companies group their customers into segments, they create programs to increase efficiency by treating customers all the same, they pay magazines and TV stations a fee to talk to their customers on their behalf, they invent policies to protect themselves from customers who might take advantage of them. The customer is thought of as an object of the company's actions, and the company sees itself as an object of the customer's actions. There is a distance created; there are barriers erected.

When you consider how little contact most executives have with actual, living, breathing customers, it's even easier to understand how these barriers come into being. The business in question may be a large consulting firm with seven-figure projects, or a fine restaurant with $40 entrées, but the interface between the company and the customer may be very similar to the convenience store and its bulletproof glass.

As Doug Ducey, CEO of Cold Stone Creamery, says, "You can't 'mail it in' and be We. You can mail it in and be Us & Them." Removing barriers between you and your customer helps you create more powerful encounters.

Consider the encounters that you have with your customers. How many are mediated, and how many are immediate? Are the mediated encounters there out of necessity, or—admit it to yourself!—are they there for your convenience? Could you increase the ratio of immediate to mediated encounters?

Your challenge is to take away the obstacles and barriers that intervene between you and your customers. The more layers you put between you and customers, the less they will be willing (and able) to really hear what you have to say. Any time there is a medium between you and your customer, you are making a compromise.

Stuart Rosenberg spent many years as the host of a show on WBEZ, the Chicago NPR affiliate. Radio is highly mediated. The airwaves, static, knobs, and dials all stand between the commentator and the listener. One person speaks to many. To feel closer to his audience, Stuart said, "I had to make the microphone go away." He wanted to feel as if nothing existed between him and his listeners.

Think this way with your customers. Ask yourself, "What can I do to be as immediate as possible? How can I reduce the inherent mediation of emails, telephones, and brochures? How can I ensure that I have enough direct encounters with my customers that the mediated interactions are seen by the customers as supplementary, and not as the main foundation of our relationship?"

> **NOTICE>>** Over the next week, in situations where you are a customer, notice the interactions and touchpoints between you and companies who sell to you. How many encounters are immediate, and how many are mediated? How often are you in a direct conversation with the "right" person, and how often are you forced to communicate through indirect channels, such as reading product literature or packaging, or talking with the "wrong" person. Is the ratio of immediate to mediated interactions appropriate, or could companies do a better job engaging your interest if they increased the number of immediate encounters?

> **HOW DO YOU COMPARE>>** Now, look at the touchpoints between you and your customers. How pure are they? How many of them are mediated by third parties

set between you and your customer, and how many are immediate? How do you stack up relative to other companies where you are a customer? Are there more, or fewer, barriers between you and your customers?

Which are most influential—for better or worse—in affecting brand impressions, the mediated or immediate interactions?

What would it take to create additional immediate encounters? Look at the mediated touchpoints between you and your customers—can you identify those where it makes sense to remove barriers and encounter your customers directly?

TRY THIS>> As you initiate encounters with customers over the next week, choose to opt for the more immediate way to communicate. If you start to email a customer, stop and pick up the phone. In another situation, instead of calling a customer, go see her in person.

ENCOUNTER ELEMENT #2: CONVERSATION

3 ELEMENTS OF AN ENCOUNTER
one: engagment in the moment
two: conversation
three: uniqueness

"THE MOST EAGER SPEAKING AT ONE ANOTHER DOES NOT MAKE A CONVERSATION." — MARTIN BUBER, *DIALOGUE* (1932)

"OBJECTIVE SPEECH SNATCHES ONLY AT A FRINGE OF REAL LIFE."
— MARTIN BUBER, *I AND THOU*

A young woman from our family, still in her teens, needed surgery. The first doctor she and her mother visited presented a very comforting and confident manner. He explained the surgery very well, describing all potential complications and options. He gave them all the information they needed. She and mom returned home assured that he was the right doctor.

On the advice of another doctor in our family, our patient also interviewed Dr. Elisa Barak Fisher, even though she was totally happy with the first doctor. The meeting with Dr.

Fisher was completely different from the appointment with the first doctor, in a way she and her mother couldn't have imagined after the first visit.

Dr. Fisher didn't just explain the surgery to her. Sure, Dr. Fisher did that—she covered all the basics. But she also asked her young patient how she felt about the surgery, and about what worried her. She listened well and expressed sincere concern and empathy. They had a conversation. The young girl told me later, "I felt like Dr. Fisher wanted to learn as much from me as I wanted to learn from her. She was the only doctor who took notes."

Marketing Beyond Storytelling— Creating Conversation

"SEEK TO UNDERSTAND AND ACKNOWLEDGE BEFORE SEEKING TO BE UNDERSTOOD AND INFLUENCE."—DR. JAY FERRARO

It has become fashionable to speak of marketing and branding in terms of storytelling. To a point, it's a workable metaphor, because customers come to understand the story of a brand over time, through a series of experiences and interactions.

> Create a conversation with your customer that becomes the story. Create the story together.

But the *telling* of a story only goes so far. Your customers are hearing many stories, from yours and many other companies, all day long. And, the sad truth is, they don't care about most of these stories. They care about their own stories.

A customer is more likely to care about your story—and, importantly, to understand your story—if you involve her in that story. Don't just tell your story to your customer. Create a conversation with your customer that becomes the story. Create the story together.

From Monologue to Dialogue

"AND THUS WHEN YOU MET SOMEONE WHO *LISTENED*, SOMEONE CONTENT TO DO NOTHING BUT, SO OVERWHELMING WAS THE DIFFERENCE, YOU HAD THE STARTLING AND QUITE LONELY EPIPHANY THAT EVERYONE ELSE, EVERY PERSON YOU'D ENCOUNTERED SINCE THE DAY YOU WERE BORN WHO'D *SUPPOSEDLY* LISTENED, HAD REALLY NOT BEEN LISTENING TO YOU AT ALL. THEY'D BEEN SUBTLY CHECKING OUT THEIR OWN REFLECTION IN THE GLASS BUREAU A LITTLE TO THE WEST OF YOUR HEAD, THINKING WHAT THEY HAD TO DO LATER THAT EVENING, OR DECIDING THAT NEXT, AS SOON AS YOU SHUT UP, THEY WERE GOING TO TELL THAT CLASSIC STORY ABOUT THEIR BOUT OF BANGLADESHI BEACHSIDE DYSENTERY, THEREBY SHOWCASING HOW WORLDLY, HOW WILD (NOT TO MENTION HOW UTTERLY ENVIABLE) A HUMAN BEING THEY WERE."**—MARISHA PESSL,** *SPECIAL TOPICS IN CALAMITY PHYSICS*

> Yes, we have to talk. But we also have to listen.

To engage customers in conversation and involve them in stories represents one of the most basic, but substantial, shifts in the way we think about marketing communications. Marketing has long been dominated by monologue—the creation of a story, the sending of messages, the writing of copy, the broadcast of images. Creating We relationships requires marketers also to see into the minds of customers by engaging in their stories, reading into the words customers say.

As a marketing term, the word "interactive," got hijacked in the early '90s to describe any type of communication that involved a computer or, more specifically, the Internet. Ironically, many of these communications were anything but interactive. In its true sense, interactive communication between sellers and buyers involves a balanced, frictionless conversation.

Simply put, we have to go beyond monological storytelling to mutual, dialogical story creation with our customers. Yes, we have to talk. But we also have to listen, and every subsequent word we say to a customer after listening to her must be informed by what we have heard.

The Three Types of Dialogue

In an essay titled "Dialogue," published several years after *I and Thou*, Martin Buber describes three types of dialogue:

> **1) Genuine Dialogue**..."in which each of the participants really has in mind the other or others in their present and particular being and turns to them with the intention of establishing a living mutual relation between himself and them."

> **2) Technical Dialogue**..."which is prompted solely by the need of objective understanding." (Think of your tech guy explaining new software.)

> **3) Monologue Disguised as Dialogue**..."characterized soley by the desire to have one's own self-reliance confirmed by marking the impression that is made."

Genuine dialogue fuels the formation of genuine encounters. It goes beyond the trading of stories to the creation of true conversation. It is like a dance, in that it is mutual and the participants are in a flow together. Ideas are shared, and, even if there is disagreement, the participants are able to understand each other, make themselves understood, and learn together. Dr. Jay Ferraro describes it as "speaking into the listening; speaking into the other person's experience of themselves, as opposed to speaking into my experiences of myself."

Technical dialogue has its necessary place in many relationships. If I were to study a musical instrument with a master, it would be possible for us to have genuine dialogue, but it would also be necessary, at other times, for him to explain technical things to me. Likewise, there are times when you and your customer must explain things to each other. The trick is only to use technical dialogue when necessary, and with awareness and intention. Understand what you are doing, and why you are doing it, and be sure to envelop technical explanations in the surroundings of genuine dialogue.

Monologue disguised as dialogue finds its way into virtually all relationships, but it is dangerous and should be avoided. As Buber writes, monologue disguised as dialogue is where "two or more men, meeting in space, speak each with himself in strangely tortuous and circuitous ways." Without consciously acknowledging it, the speakers of monologue disguised as dialogue are actually speaking more to themselves than to others.

> **Monologue disguised as dialogue is the poison of marketing and sales communications.**

Monologue disguised as dialogue is the poison of marketing and sales communications (let alone of marriages and political bodies). Think of how often someone is intent on telling you something and, like a bulldozer, he proceeds without any sense of how you are reacting to his speech. It is as if he planned to deliver this peroration long before he met with you, and he is going to deliver it no matter what. Direct marketing, scripted customer service interactions, infomercials, most sales pitches—all of these are monologue disguised as dialogue. They all offer a "call to action," but they are all nothing but the delivery of a "shpiel." Once in a while the customer will respond to the shpiel, but most of the time the customer won't even notice the volley of communication.

Why I Don't Believe in the "Elevator Pitch"

> **The biggest problem with creating an elevator pitch is that you may actually tell it to someone.**

The concept of the "elevator pitch" has become popular in recent years. An elevator pitch is what you would say if you were lucky enough to find yourself in an elevator for 30 seconds with the CEO of a prospective client company. You can think of it as a short, succinct description of who you are and why you matter. The exercise of writing your elevator pitch is valuable to the extent that it helps you figure out what you stand for. But it is dangerous to embrace the concept of the elevator pitch literally, because you may actually tell it to someone. Why focus on creating the perfect 30-second monologue? Why not focus on developing the tools for creating the perfect 30-second dialogue? That way, you'll be prepared to create it on the spot. You'll have a much better chance of being invited to continue the conversation with the CEO at a later time.

Steve Pinetti, senior vice president of marketing and sales for Kimpton Hotels & Restaurants, describes what this looks like from the customer's perspective. "In my job, people are always trying to sell me products and services. But 99 percent of salespeople who call me on the phone or send me an email start talking about their product and why it is so great. They 'feature dump.' I don't buy from them, meet with them, or even return their calls or emails. But if somebody reaches out to me and it's clear they've done their research, and then they really listen, it opens the door for the dialogue. That's very few people, but those are the ones I meet with." By engaging in dialogue, a good salesperson can learn what Steve wants, and focus the conversation on what's relevant. The other salespeople come armed with their elevator pitch, and feel compelled to use it. It would be sheer coincidence if their monologue connected with him.

One of the best ways to create genuine dialogue is to avoid delivering monologue disguised as dialogue.

Stop Targeting

> "WE'RE ATTACKING THE TARGET MARKET WITH A
> RIFLE SHOT APPROACH."

> "WE'RE IN A FIERCE BATTLE WITH THE COMPETITION TO
> CAPTURE MARKET SHARE."

> "WE'VE SCHEDULED A VOLLEY OF ADVERTISING FOR
> THE FALL."

I've actually heard people say these things. What is this, marketing, or West Point?

Why are we targeting customers? Are we trying to shoot them?

These are marketing words I avoid:

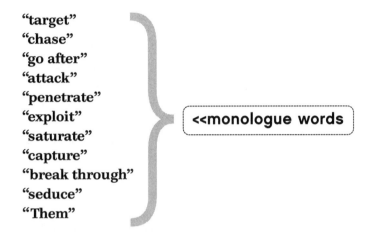

"target"
"chase"
"go after"
"attack"
"penetrate"
"exploit"   <<monologue words
"saturate"
"capture"
"break through"
"seduce"
"Them"

These are marketing words I love:

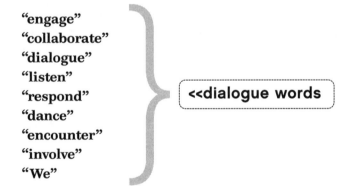

"engage"
"collaborate"
"dialogue"
"listen"
"respond"   <<dialogue words
"dance"
"encounter"
"involve"
"We"

Throwing information at customers is a very ineffective method of communication. If I want to persuade you of something, would I have much luck if I tried to "capture" you or "target" you?

Marketing is not hypnosis. Is it not something you do *to* your customers. It is something you do *with* them.

The Lessons of Socrates

> **Socrates never tells a person what to think.**

Socrates did not leave behind any of his own writings. All we know of his teaching is given in a series of *Dialogues* published by his student, Plato. In these dialogues, Plato recounts conversations between Socrates and others. In each case, the person with whom Socrates engages in dialogue comes to important realizations. Socrates never tells the person what to think. His conversational style helps the other arrive at a place where he can tell himself what to think.

People often describe Socratic dialogue as a series of questions. But this sells it short; Socrates does much more than ask questions. He engages the person with whom he is talking in a genuine conversation that helps the other person realize important things for himself.

This is the essence of a productive, mutual dialogue with a customer. A customer will connect with your message much better if she comes to conclusions for herself in the course of productive dialogue with you. This is much more effective communication than trying to convince her of something through monologue.

These important things, which the customer can decide, might include…

- Whether to be in the conversation with you

- Whether to share information with you

- Whether to commit to the moment fully

- How to think about you

- How to think about the subject matter of the conversation

We live in an age of empowered customers who passionately reserve the right to think for themselves. This is true of all aspects of their relationship with you, including the right to decide whether to engage with you. The true lesson of Socrates is that there are genuine, productive ways to engage a person in a conversation in which that person will come to believe, for herself, things that you would like to communicate.

"Yes, and"— A Conversation Can Have Many Paths

Earlier I described a conversation with clients that didn't go well. I wanted to go straight to the "meat" of the conversation but they felt a need to talk first about some irritating political problems our project was having in their company. I related that I didn't handle the conversation very well because I said "No" to the direction my clients wanted to take.

While recounting that story, I described how actors improvising on stage use a technique called "Yes, and" to advance a scene. The idea is never to say "No" to what another actor does or says, but to use what they say as a springboard for your next comment. "Yes" propels a scene forward, "No" kills it. This is a very effective conversational strategy. Had I said, "Yes, and here's what I suggest we do about it…," my clients would have become engaged with me in the conversation. After that, it would have been easier to move to my topic.

Do not try to force a customer conversation. Do not be tied to your specific agenda. Get the customer engaged, and keep them engaged through a process of "Yes, and." Everything your customer says becomes an opportunity to move the conversation forward, and once you are engaged with your customer he will be willing to travel with you to your destination.

> Karyn Kedar describes one of the most important types of conversations she has in her job as a rabbi: the meeting with a family prior to a funeral. "People don't know where to start, so I tell them, 'start in the middle.' Then, I begin to look for the thread that connects together the life of the loved one who has died. It is not important what order they tell me stories in. In fact, if I were to force them into an order, it's likely that I wouldn't ever hear the real story. People want to take a random walk through their issues, so I let them. I give them permission to talk."

> **What is important is that you and your customer are engaged on a path, after which you can find the right path and identify the right destination.**

The exact path your conversation takes is not important. What is most important is that you and your customer are engaged on a path, after which you can find the right path and identify the right destination. Forcing your customer down your exact path might shut them down. Help them get into a conversation, in whatever way works best for them, and then they will be more likely to travel with you to your desired destination.

Joe Honor, vice president of VMC Behavioral Health Care Services, a provider of Employee Assistance Programs, describes a situation that happened during a presentation to a client. "We were in the middle of a presentation to a prospective client, when the client asked a question that was unrelated to the content we were covering. I stopped the presentation and asked him, 'This sounds like something that really matters to you. Can we stop for a minute? Tell me what's important to you.' As he described the problem he was having, I asked him a number of questions to help me understand his situation. At first, our conversation seemed like a tangent, and I could tell that my colleagues were a little worried about my departure from our agenda. But the client got very interested in the conversation, and, at one point, I said, 'Based on what you're saying, I have an idea. Do you want to hear something innovative?' I had learned enough from the conversation to offer him an idea that hadn't been part of our presentation. That led to an even deeper conversation, and it helped us sell a significantly larger product that we had expected to sell. Not only did we make the sale and start a great relationship with that client, the idea led to an entire new product line for our company. Three years later this is one of our strongest customer relationships."

As Joe tells me this story I think of the times a presenter, unwilling and unable to depart from his PowerPoint slide show, deflects audience questions that are off topic. "We'll get to that," they say, or, "That's not what we're covering now, but we'll get to it later." Joe was willing to step back and let the sales presentation become a conversation. Dealing with tangential comments and questions can be tough, but the payoff for handling them is great.

Tacking: Keeping a Conversation On Track

Once you start a conversation with someone, you want to keep it moving in a positive direction. However, it is often difficult to keep a conversation on track. The other person has many distractions, and many places to which his mind can wander. Rabbi Karyn Kedar and I were talking about keeping a conversation on track, and she used a metaphor from sailing:

KARYN: It's like tacking when you're sailing.

STEVE: What do you mean?

KARYN: Well, You never sail straight. You always sail in a zig-zag because, at any given moment, the environment is changing so you have to readjust your sails, and reposition the boat in order to catch the wind. That's called tacking. So when you're in an encounter, you have to do a series of check-ins to see if you've lost the person you are in dialogue with. And if you have lost them, then you have to re-invite either by your eyes or the modulation of your voice or your body movement. You have to re-engage, re-invite into the moment.

STEVE: So you constantly need to re-invite somebody in, even if they're engaged.

KARYN: You have to check the wind to see where they've gone, if they're with you, or if they're not with you.

STEVE: And even if they're with you, there's an opportunity to catch even more wind. If you're sailing and things are going great, sometimes you can adjust the tack, and get a much better wind.

KARYN: Right, because you're alert to how the conversation is going. You are in the moment. You're thinking. It's not a story line that you're giving through rote. You are in the moment.

> A conversation must be monitored and nutured for its duration.

If you've ever sailed, you know the wonderful feeling of the wind, the sheets (ropes) and the tiller, all in tension, as you balance all forces to ride the wind in the best way possible. Sailing is never static, never constant. You are continuously alert as you adjust the sails, whether it is to avoid slowing down or to take advantage of an opportunity to catch more wind and increase your speed.

A conversation is much like this. As described earlier, many of the conversations Rabbi Kedar has with her congregants are tough conversations about critical life events. She is acutely aware that conversation requires ongoing alertness and adjustment. We all experience something similar in our business conversations. A conversation must be monitored and nurtured for its duration.

In *The Philadelphia Story* (1940) Katherine Hepburn's character, Tracy Lord, describes a favorite sailboat to Cary Grant's character, C. K. Dexter Haven: *"My, she was yar...It means, easy to handle, quick to the helm, fast, right. Everything a boat should be."* Keeping a conversation *yar*, like a sailboat that is quick and agile, is something to strive for in all encounters.

Imagine a conversation between you and a customer that is yar, where the customer feels that you respond like an agile racing boat, skimming over the water, buoyed by the wind. Wouldn't this be a powerful encounter?

Managing the Out of Balance Conversation

Genuine dialogue does not require each party to say half the words.

Every month or two I meet a certain client for breakfast, and I know what to expect. He sees the meeting as a chance to update me on the status of his business, and I can predict with certainty that

> **One of the surest ways to let an interaction slide from the world of encounter to the realm of transaction is to talk AT your customer for 10 minutes straight.**

he will do 90 percent of the talking in the first 45 minutes we are together. But we always have a great conversation.

I listen carefully, and I make sure that the few words I say are informed by what he is saying. I don't try to change the flow of the conversation, but I am an active participant in it. Like the sailor on a good tack, my adjustments are subtle. Personally, I really like this kind of conversations with customers. I learn a lot about my clients, and, generally, most people like to be listened to. It's a pretty easy way to make a customer happy.

The flipside of this is the situation where you *have* to do most of the talking. For example, there are times when you have to explain something to a customer, and the customer expects you to do most of the talking, as we described earlier with Buber's concept of technical dialogue. It is challenging to create dialogue in these moments, and easy to slip into monologue. One of the surest ways to let an interaction slide from the world of encounter to the realm of transaction is to talk at your customer for 10 minutes straight.

Personally, this latter situation is where I have to watch myself. As much as I love conversation, I also love to explain things to people. If I'm not vigilant, I'll default to talking fast, delivering an enormous amount of information, hardly pausing to take a breath. To avoid this tendency of monologue, I keep in mind the three elements of an encounter, engagement in the moment, conversation, and unique-ness, (which we will discuss in depth below). As I deliver information to my customer, I look for ways to invite him into the moment. I try to be conscious of moving at a pace that he is comfortable with. I look for opportunities to ask him questions and create dialogue—it's easy for someone to space out when they have to listen for a long time.

Help Them Say What They Can't Say

> **Your challenge is to tap into the other's knowing, to find the wisdom and beliefs that are inside them and, through conversation, help them say what they might not otherwise be able to say.**

People know more than they are able to say. This is especially true if you are engaging a customer in a conversation about a topic with which you have deep familiarity, but they have not put much thought into. For example, I consult with companies about their core brand values, something to which many have never given more than a passing thought. Even though a person may not have the vocabulary or clearly developed thoughts about a subject to articulate a complete set of ideas, they are incredibly knowledgeable about their companies. The ideas are there. We just have to thread them together into a sensible conversation.

Your challenge is to tap into the other's knowing, to find the wisdom and beliefs that are inside him and, through conversation, help him say what he might not otherwise be able to say.

People are often passionate about things they cannot articulate. Additionally, they often cannot express their anxieties in direct ways, as we saw with our discussion of "aboutism." However, if you listen closely and are deeply engaged with a customer in a conversation, you will understand what they want to say even though they haven't said it. Then, you can help them say it. That would be a productive dialogue.

> Think perspicuity:
> How can I make myself better understood?
> Think perspicacity:
> How can I more easily understand?

Clarity and Alertness: Perspicuity and Perspicacity

To be a good communicator, you have to both understand and be understood. Here is a wonderful set of words to describe this, that are sorely underused by speakers of English:

Perspicuity   Perspicacity

A **perspicuous** person is one who can make himself clearly understood.

A **perspicacious** person is one who is acutely perceptive, with penetrating discernment.

These two qualities can contribute to good conversation. They are especially valuable to you if your customer either lacks them or is unwilling to be clear or acutely perceptive in the conversation.

If you are perspicuous, you will be easily understood, even by the customer who is not very alert or engaged. Perspicuity is enhanced by clarity, and communicating with a customer in a way that is particularly relevant to him.

If you are perspicacious, you will easily understand your customer, even if she is not very articulate or forthcoming with information. Perspicacity is enhanced by alertness, when you see meaning in the most subtle cues revealed by your customer.

NOTICE>> As a customer, how many companies in the course of a week engage you in true conversations? Think of many different types of interactions you have, from buying a cup of coffee or ordering a meal to purchases you make on the job. Are sellers talking at you, or conversing with you?

HOW DO YOU COMPARE>> How do you and your organization compare? How regularly do you engage your customers in dialogue, and how often do you talk at them?

What are the obstacles in your organization that prevent dialogue? What systems or conventions encourage monologue? How can you increase the chances of dialogue?

> **TRY THIS>>** As you interact with people, be conscious of the degree of dialogue that takes place.

● Notice whether you and the other person are in conversation, or in parallel monologues.

● As you converse, look for the ways your comments connect to the other person's comments. How does he react to what you say?

● Monitor the status of the conversation, looking for opportunities to "tack" and "catch a better wind."

● Be aware of people who practice monologue disguised as dialogue, and, as you talk with them, search for subtle ways to encourage them to engage in conversation.

ENCOUNTER ELEMENT #3: UNIQUENESS

3 ELEMENTS OF AN ENCOUNTER
one: engagment in the moment
two: conversation
three: uniqueness

Invent Each Encounter for This Moment

I walk into Blockbuster Video, and the door makes a chime. The employee working behind the counter shouts, "Welcome to Blockbuster. How are you today?" with his back turned to the door—and to my face.

Freshness

Isn't it obvious when someone pushes "play" on their internal audio player and begins talking to you with words that seem pre-recorded? You hear them talk, and you know that they have said these same words to other people, at other times. A salesman spouts his "shpiel"…a restaurant hostess delivers a Pavlovian greeting as soon as she sees you walk through the door…30 minutes later, after your meal is delivered, the waiter asks perfunctorily, "Is everything okay?"

A true encounter never feels like this. It feels as if it is being invented for this moment, as the first of its kind. As you experience it, you believe that this encounter has never happened before in the entire history of the universe. It does not feel as if it has been pulled "off the rack."

> Great encounters have a feeling of spontaneity, created with the freshness of an improvised John Coltrane solo.

Great encounters have a feeling of spontaneity, created with the freshness of an improvised John Coltrane saxophone solo. The encounter may have been considered beforehand, but any agenda is transparent. If there is an agenda, it is only a guideline. It serves the encounter, providing a framework for spontaneity, but does not limit the encounter. Experience and training guide you as you create an encounter, but they do not script you. Even when you encounter a customer with whom you have had many interactions, it is

> No matter what the interaction is, it is always possible to make it less formulaic and less scripted.

important to treat this encounter as unique and worthy of unique design. Your 100th meeting with a customer should be a one-of-a-kind meeting that has never happened before and will never happen again.

This is, no doubt, easier in some businesses than in others. A psychiatrist with a patient on the couch for an hour certainly has an easier setting for a one-of-a-kind encounter than does a McDonald's employee during the busy lunch rush. However, regardless of the setting, it is *always* possible to make it less formulaic and less scripted. Earlier today, I was speaking with a client who runs a commercial real estate operation, with office buildings across the country. We had an interesting conversation about the possibility of creating an encounter in a twenty-second chance meeting in the lobby with a tenant. Our conclusion: Yes. You can take a simple, short meeting and turn it into a special moment, one that has never occurred before, and one that will never occur again. You can make a tenant feel that this short meeting in the lobby was created at this moment, for this moment.

Repetition Doesn't Have to Kill Freshness

Through experimentation, I have found a few strategies for making repetitive situations stay fresh. In conversations with my friends and clients, I consciously try to say things in ways I've never said them before. This is difficult, especially in business, because we have so many conversations over and over, about the same set of topics. It is easy to fall into the trap of pulling everything you say "from inventory." So I try, especially with topics I've discussed frequently, to find new ways to present them every time. New adjectives, a new word order, a new order for citing examples, new metaphors if any come to mind; for me, this helps keep things fresh. I also use this in public speaking. I do about fifty speeches and presentations every year, and, like all speakers, I have a large bank of stories and examples to draw from. But if I pull a story from this bank, I always try to tell it in a new way, even if I've told it many times before. Otherwise, it can sound recycled.

I asked Roslyn Alexander, the actress I wrote about earlier in this book, "How is it possible to sound fresh, even if you've delivered the same lines or told the story many times before?" She offered some interesting perspectives:

> The experience will always seem like a new experience if you recognize what makes it new. People often ask me, "How can you play that same run, night after night, saying the same lines in each performance? It's all the same." I answer that it is not the same thing. You're different than you were yesterday, the other actors are different than they were yesterday, the audience is different, the environment is different—you'll sound different if it is colder on the stage tonight than it was last night. If you observe the differences and are aware of them, your performance will be fresh because you will be responding to the differences around you.

If you are alert to the uniqueness of the moment that is already in progress, it is easier to craft a fresh encounter. Be alert to the setting. As I am talking with someone, I try to be alert to the room we are in, the ambience, the mood, the temperature, etc. Some people might find this distracting, but I find that this alertness not only gets me into the moment, it awakens me to what makes this particular time and place special. I see that this situation and this set of circumstances could not have ever existed before. If the scene seems common to me, the interaction may also seem common to me—and then, I may seem common. Last week, I went to a breakfast meeting at a restaurant I've been to at least 100 times. I wasn't very excited about this particular meeting, so I ordered something off the menu that I had never ordered before, to see if this helped make the moment unique. It worked. Noticing the new taste and the new meal presentation added a note of freshness to the meeting. It made it easier for me to engage with this person in a way I had never engaged before.

If you want to see each new encounter with a person as unique, even if you have met with that person many times before, be alert to what makes today's meeting special. Today, I saw the connection between the uniqueness of each encounter and my love for the beach in South Haven, Michigan. My wife's family has owned a cottage on a bluff overlooking Lake Michigan since 1927, where I am now writing this passage. I have spent weekends and getaway vacations here for 26 years, and I hike down the stairs to the beach multiple times every day that I am here. I have seen this beach on picture-perfect summer days, and during winter storms. I have loved it at one o'clock in the afternoon and one o'clock in the morning. I have been enjoying sunsets from this beach for 26 years, and I have learned to see the special beauty in each one.

Some evenings our sunsets offer an arabesque of clouds. The different shades of light are reflected off them and refracted through them as the sun sets. The sky on these nights is a spectacle, with the kind of sunsets people tell their friends about. I watch the horizon as the colors change through different degrees of magnificence, and the evening transforms into night.

On other evenings, when there are few clouds and the weather is still, I'm fascinated by the small area around the setting sun and the trail of color on the water leading all the way from there to here. As the sun wanes, the true beauty is the water, where the ripples become pastel patterns of purple and pink. These sunsets are subtle. If I am waiting for the overpowering, breathtaking, grand gestures of the spectacular sunsets described above, I will be disappointed. But, if I am tuned in to the softer displays in the rippling water, and I listen for the music of the small surf hitting the beach, I can appreciate that the beauty of this sunset is every bit as awe-inspiring as that of its spectacular sister. It just has to be appreciated in a different way.

This is how we can see the uniqueness in the successive encounters we have with a customer over time. Some meetings are like the powerful sunset; a major presentation that includes creative brainstorming with your customer, or a time when you both sign a contract for a new project. It is easy to notice the significance of these meetings. But there are other meetings whose messages may be as subtle as the pink and purple ripples on the water. A short phone call, a chance meeting with a client on the street, a casual lunch. Stay alert to the beauty and significance in the subtleties of these encounters;

they can contribute some of the richest enhancements to your grow-ing relationship.

The moment is unique. Acknowledge that it is.

How Process Can Get in the Way of Uniqueness

> **It would have been impossible for their employees to provide good service if they had obeyed the rules.**

Service businesses are notorious for providing thorough training for their employees. They teach their employees a detailed, exhaustive set of processes for doing their jobs, and then they measure employee performance by how well the employees comply with the system. One com-pany I worked with taught their employees a 38-step process for completing a 5-minute customer transaction. (I was relieved to learn through research that most employees were unaware of these steps. It would have been impossible for them to provide good service if they obeyed the rules.) There is, of course, a need to teach service employees how to provide a basic level of service and to perform necessary proce-dures and actions. But the point is not to confuse procedures with unique, special customer encounters. Consistency is fine when you are talking about how the cashier operates a cash register. But con-sistency is a negative when you talk about how the same cashier interacts with a customer. Consistency is highly overrated.

Policy can be the enemy of uniqueness. Yes, policies and proce-dures are necessary for the running of a business. But, be aware of the problems they can cause. A policy designed to ensure that all customers get consistent, similar service ensures just that: All customers will get the same service, and personalization will be blunted. A policy that ensures that all your employees relate to cus-tomers in the same way ensures that your employees will be more formulaic and less likely to engage with customers in a way that seems relevant to both employee *and* customer.

If employees are taught to base their customer interactions on outcomes, with process used only as guidance and not as constraint, they will surprise you with their ingenuity in getting to those out-

A policy designed to ensure that all customers get consistent service ensures that personalization will be blunted.

comes. Consistency is okay if it forms a strong foundation that allows unique encounters to occur. But that is just the starting point. Ideally, policies and procedures should liberate and support employees, helping them to create unique encounters.

Niki Leondakis, chief operating officer for Kimpton Hotels & Restaurants, says that customers value personalized treatment because they don't receive it very often. "We're so used to not being related to as individuals that we expect to be slapped down if we need something out of the ordinary. 'I have this individual need, and you're going to give me some version of a policy.' As customers we believe that companies make it hard for their employees to personalize."

Niki believes that employees acting outside the constraints of policy can actually enhance a customer's relationship with a brand. "When I'm dealing with somebody paid by the hour, and they do something extraordinary, like they leave their workstation to take care of me and do something outside the norm of their job...when I see that, now I have a relationship with the company, because somebody higher up is supporting his doing that. Culturally, that's encouraged and allowed. It's happening at a bigger level." She tells stories of how such a culture is nurtured at Kimpton Hotels. "We encourage our employees to get creative to help guests, and some of the best examples happen when guests show up late at night after a bad travel experience. A guest checked into one of our hotels in Chicago, really frazzled, and he started asking our bellman where he could get some food. He didn't want anything on our menu, but really wanted some Chinese food. The bellman explained where the nearest Chinese restaurant was, but could see that the guest was really tired. The bellman took the guest up to his room, and then ran out to get the Chinese food for him. No permission needed. He knew he was allowed to do it. We had another new front desk employee in Boston, who was checking in a guest late at night after a long flight delay.

> **It is important that the customer can see that the employee is "obviously empowered" to personalize the interaction if it will enhance the customer's relationship with the brand.**

She told the guest about our complimentary evening wine hour. He seemed very interested in the wine hour, but had arrived too late for it this evening, and was leaving too soon the next day. After he went to his room she asked her supervisor if it was okay to give the guest a bottle of wine, since he'd miss the wine hour. The supervisor said, 'Of course, if you want to do it, do it.' 'Don't I need permission?' 'No.' 'Don't I have to fill out paperwork?' 'No.' She sent him a bottle of wine with a note that said, 'Sorry you had such a hard time getting here.' He was delighted, and she used this story to tell her manager why she loved her job. I am convinced that when our guests see our employees going outside their normal job to help them, that translates to a better relationship with the brand."

Niki adds that it's important that the customer can see that the employee is "obviously empowered" to personalize the interaction if it will enhance the customer's relationship with the brand. She relates one of her own experiences with an airline: "I was on an airplane, sitting in the first row of coach, just behind first class. I ended up talking to the first class flight attendant, and he offered me a glass of wine. I wasn't really interested in it, but I took it because I was so surprised that he would offer it to me. But it didn't make me like the airline any more, because I knew he was breaking the rules. I'm certain they don't recognize and support employees who go outside the norm to help a customer."

If a company is policy-heavy, as is an airline, the customer will not expect to be treated like an individual, and the occasional individual treatment will seem like an aberration, provided by a single employee. The brand experience created by an airline is more about rules and process than it is about making each customer happy. "I knew that what he did was his personal act of kindness. There are too many situations where that doesn't happen. I don't believe it's the airline saying, 'Do these kinds of things for people,'" says Niki. But if an employee's personalized encounter with a customer is res-onant with other parts of the customer experience, the employee's actions will reinforce the overall brand experience. "When it happens with different individuals," Niki adds, "now you really see that it's not just one person, it's the company. There's something going on here that's right. These people actually care about me and respect me."

NOTICE>> Grab a small notebook and carry it with you for the next week. As a customer, note when encounters seem invented for you or pre-scripted. How do they make you feel? What are the outcomes for the pre-scripted vs. the invented encounters?

HOW DO YOU COMPARE>> Now, rate your organization. Do you provide routine, recycled experiences for customers, or one-of-a-kind encounters? Where do your most scripted transactions occur?

TRY THIS>> Next time you are in a situation you've been in many times before, look for ways to make it different. Order something new at your favorite restaurant. Tell a story in a new way, using new words or new examples. Say something to a good friend that you've never said to him or her before. Take any script you rely on and abandon it. Pay attention to how newness creates freshness. What other routines can you break?

TRY THIS>> Look at some routine touchpoints between you and your customers. Look for ways to reduce routine and scripting. What can you do to turn these interactions into unique encounters?

Could Only Have Been Us: We Are Both Irreplaceable

When interacting with you, how valuable would it be if your customer were to think, "This encounter could only happen with the two of us. With someone else, it would be different." What if you were both irreplaceable in the encounter?

Can you think of an encounter you have had where the success of that encounter depended on the specific participation of you and the other person involved? What about an experience in a restaurant where a waiter's special personality added to the experience, and where that waiter keyed in on your personality and engaged you in a way that reflected his understanding of you? Think of an encounter with one of your customers that would have been totally different if two other people had been involved. This customer may buy products like yours from other people, but the way the two of you interact is different from how he interacts with your competitors. Similarly, you have many customers, but the way you interact with this customer is different from your interactions with all other customers. While both of you may have wonderful encounters with other people, your encounters together are unique because of the participation of the two of you.

"Irreplaceable" means that there could be no substitute for either of you in this encounter without vastly changing it. It means that your participation makes the encounter unique. And, moreover, it means that your customer feels that the moment is uniquely created for him.

It is obvious to a customer when you give him a generic message that could have been given to any other customer. But, he will be more likely to perceive an interaction as an encounter, as opposed to a transaction, if he knows that this encounter was invented specially *just for him.*

Creating a personal encounter with a customer is one of the best competitive strategies available to you. Experiences can be copied by competitors. But a competitor cannot duplicate the private encounters you have with an individual customer.

When you see the customer as unique and irreplaceable, and the customer sees you as unique and irreplaceable, together you can create a unique and irreplaceable relationship.

For either of you, a transaction could have happened with someone else.

But an encounter could only have happened with the two of you.

How to Make Each of You Irreplaceable in the Encounter

The key to making you both irreplaceable in the encounter is to ensure that you both participate as full, unique human beings—not as representatives of a particular job function. In a transaction, you interact with a categorical function: "Toll taker." "Motorist." "Convenience store cashier." "The twentieth person to buy a cup of coffee in the last hour." In an encounter you interact first as humans, and your respective categorical functions are only subsets of your exclusive identities.

If a customer thinks of me as a "marketing consultant," I am inherently replaceable. When he thinks of me first as "Steve," and only secondarily as a marketing consultant, it is easier to see me as unique and irreplaceable. This is something I think about: I want my clients to think of me as "Steve, our marketing consultant," and not, "our marketing consultant, Steve."

Understanding—and having confidence in—your own uniqueness is a critical first step to understanding and appreciating the uniqueness of another person. As Dr. Jay Ferraro said in our interview, "If I have grounding in who I am, I will then be able to perceive the uniqueness in you."

Believe This Person Is a Unique Human Being

Long before he wrote a biography of Martin Buber, Maurice Friedman chose to write his doctoral thesis at The University of Chicago on Buber's philosophy. Buber agreed to help Friedman on his thesis, but, as a condition of his cooperation, Buber first wanted Friedman to write an account of his own life, "without withholding and without analysis." Buber was saying that he would be better able to help the doctoral student write about his, Buber's, philosophy if he understood the student as a human being.

I love that story. I imagine that most philosophers would be so self-obsessed about their body of work that they would see a doctoral thesis like this only in terms of that body of work. Buber saw beyond himself and saw Friedman the person as indispensable to the process. He realized that the thesis was as dependent on the doctoral student writing it as it was on Buber.

In order to create an encounter, you must interact with a customer in a way that acknowledges his extraordinary uniqueness as the only person who has ever lived his life before. This is not our natural inclination. We are more likely to associate a new acquaintance with a category of other people "just like him" than we are to create a "category of one" that includes only him.

Think what happens when you meet a new person. From the very first instant, you notice things about this person. Man or woman? What age? Height, size, hair color, etc.

It is natural, as you learn these things, to categorize this person based on characteristics of people you've met before. Within seconds of meeting someone, you have conveniently placed them into a bucket that might have the name "Skateboarding teenagers who dress with rebellion," or "Bearded college professors who drive Volvos."

We learned to make generalizations like this millions of years ago. Our ancestors would encounter animals on the Pleistocene savannah and have to think, immediately, "Predator or prey?" "Wants to kill me or doesn't want to kill me?" "Smells like danger or doesn't smell like danger?" "Looks like it would taste good or looks like it would taste disgusting?" And for the people we'd meet, we had to think, "Friend or foe?' "Kin or enemy?" "Stronger than I am or weaker?"

We have to generalize in order to survive. Life is too complicated to assess every thing or person we come across, as if it were a one-

> This propensity to categorize is important, but dangerous.

of-a-kind, never-before-seen, 15-billion-years-since-the-big-bang-and-this-is-the-first-time-it-ever-happened kind of thing. By the time we would have assessed the situation, the predator would be ready for dessert.

For most people we meet, lumping them into a category is a necessity. For example, for speakers of certain languages, it is critical to decide, rather quickly, whether the person to be addressed is male or female. For a security guard in a department store, it is crucial to waste no time deciding if an out-of-place person fits into the category of "lost child crying for mommy," or "another shoplifter."

But this urge to put people into categories is such a labor-saving device that we have decided to use it with virtually all people we meet, and in most situations. When we meet a genuinely interesting person, we often miss seeing how interesting she is because we mentally toss her into a metaphysical drawer along with people "just like her." Her interesting, distinctive characteristics are obscured behind an opaque curtain formed by our preconceived notions about what she must be like. This propensity to categorize is important, but dangerous.

As for our business relationships, everything we have learned about marketing has taught us tricks to "save" us from having to think of each customer as an exceptional individual. Most techniques of customer segmentation are really nothing more than techniques for dividing a customer population into a manageable number of supposedly homogeneous groups. Demographic generalizations facilitate convenient advertising decisions, but they are a significant compromise when it comes to creating relationship-building encounters with unique customers. Businesses have invented many ways *not* to think of customers as individuals, because it is much more convenient and efficient to lump customers together and work with approximations of who they are. (As a society, we've already decided that segregation, stereotypes, and generalizations based on appearance are a bad thing. Why do businesses persist in the tradition?)

> To have a true, human encounter with someone, you must resist the temptation to dilute your understanding of her true nature and her interesting features by "averaging them out."

Businesses turn customers into abstractions and statistics, and many never really get to know their customers as distinct human beings. For many businesses, customers are an indistinguishable mass of humanity. Bureaucracy and process eclipse the true customer.

To have a true, human encounter with someone, you must resist the temptation to dilute your understanding of her true nature and her interesting features by "averaging them out" with those of other, superficially similar people. Instead of understanding her as a person that fits nicely into a predetermined category ("there are 7 billion people on this planet, and she fits into this one subset of 5 million people who are similar to her"), understand her personality and essence by first noting the details that make her special. Identify those seemingly small, yet important, flavors and spices that tell you interesting things about her character, and use those details as a foundation from which to build a unique, one-of-a-kind person in your mind.

Retail businesses often attempt to train their employees to "read the customer." This is an admirable goal, but the training often aims in the wrong direction. Typically, this training teaches employees to look for broad, generic characteristics that help the employee sort the customer into a large group of (supposedly) similar customers. While broad categorizations, such as age, gender, and clothing style, can give the employee a place to start, these characteristics can be misleading if the employee stops there. Truly reading a customer means getting beyond demographic generalities and seeing what makes this customer a distinctive human being.

When you meet someone, enter the encounter with the full, confident, heartfelt belief that the person you are meeting is an interesting, one-of-a-kind person. Be curious about this person. Enter the encounter with "new eyes," and a true appreciation of how special it is to be human, and how special this person must be. Be alert. Notice things that could possibly only exist in this person, not the things that she shares with 100 million other people.

> **NOTICE>>** As a customer, notice over the next week how often you are treated as a unique individual and how often you are treated in a cookie-cutter fashion, as if you were just another customer.

> **HOW DO YOU COMPARE>>** How does your organization rate in comparison to what you notice about how you are treated? Do you tend to recognize people as unique human beings, or does your organization interact with most people as generic customers?

Real Life Points in This Direction

> Notice things that differentiate, not things that approximate.

Next time you are in a crowded restaurant, or a busy airport terminal, look at the faces of people you don't know. Every face will be new to you, a face you have never seen before. Yes, one woman might look somewhat like a person you work with, and some guy might be "that type," but you have never seen that exact face before. Every one is special and distinctive. And that only considers the uniqueness of their looks. Imagine if you got below the surface and got to know any of these people well. Looks are only the smallest implications of uniqueness.

There are billions of people on earth, and each one is unique. We know that being human is a special, miraculous thing. We are all inherently exceptional. So are our customers.

When you are open to sensing the uniqueness of another human being, and when you are ready to accept him fully for what he is and not for what he approximates, you will notice and appreciate the details that make this person matchless and inimitable.

> We are defined not by the many things that make us similar, but by the few spices and flavors that make each of us different.

Spices and Flavors: The Small Cues to a Person's Uniqueness

We are defined not by the many things that make us similar, but by the few spices and flavors that make each of us different.

These spices and flavors, though seemingly small, make big differences between people. It doesn't take much to make someone unique. Consider that chimpanzees and humans share 98 percent of our genetic material. A very small portion of who we are makes up the difference between chimps and us. And we share 99.5 percent of our DNA with each other. We are all the same, but for the last one-half of one percent. The details make the difference. Getting to know the last half percent of a person is what it means to know "a full human being."

This is the irony: To see someone as "a full human being," you really have to recognize the smallest part of him—the fine details of his character. What makes a full human being is that last one-half percent that makes us each unique.

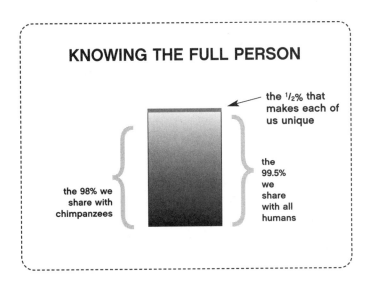

KNOWING THE FULL PERSON

the 1/2% that makes each of us unique

the 99.5% we share with all humans

the 98% we share with chimpanzees

> **You do not have to learn to be a connoisseur of people. You already are.**

The fine details that make us each unique could include physical features, as mentioned, but, more interestingly, could include quirks of character, a distinctive portfolio of interests, a singular way of thinking about things and approaching problems, a one-of-a-kind sense of humor, an interesting family history, a room-shaking laugh.

Connoisseurs—be it of wine, food, tulips, or 1950s lunchboxes—can spot the details no one else can spot in their chosen area of interest. They see beyond the generalizations to the subtleties that make a particular example special. Although we may not recognize it, we are all capable of being discerning connoisseurs of people. We could all easily add to the list in the previous paragraph, identifying other ways people can be distinctive. You do not have to learn to be a connoisseur of people. You already are. You only have to develop the habit of using the talent you already have in your business encounters.

Another way to look at it: Approach your understanding of your customers the way you come to understand a character in a piece of fiction. The best characters are those with the most interesting array of fine details, not those with one-dimensional cartoon-like personalities. Be willing to see and appreciate the characters you encounter during your work.

The Long Tail and Individuality

"CONSUMERS'...TASTES ARE FAR MORE DIVERSE THAN THE MARKETING PLANS BEING FIRED AT THEM SUGGEST."— **CHRIS ANDERSON,** *THE LONG TAIL*

Chris Anderson's 2006 book, *The Long Tail*, demonstrates how people's individuality is expressed when it is not constrained by the product choices offered in a traditional setting. The idea of *The Long Tail* is this: We have developed a "hit culture" that overvalues top sellers because our market has long been based on scarcity of shelf space, production, and distribution. Back when TV consisted of three major networks, limited airtime required a focus on hits. If a Blockbuster

Video store can stock only 3,000 of the more than 200,000 films available, it is critical that they stock the most popular movies. Similarly, Wal-Mart, America's largest music retailer, must focus only on top-selling titles, since they stock only 750 of the 30,000 albums released each year. However, when the constraints of physical inventory are taken away, as they are with Netflix or online music retailer Rhapsody, we see that people's interests go well beyond the hits. Thus, 21 percent of Netflix rentals come from titles not stocked in retail outlets, and 40 percent of Rhapsody sales come from titles not stocked in retail stores. Similarly, as Anderson points out, the average Borders store stocks 100,000 books, but 25 percent of Amazon's sales come from outside its top 100,000 titles.[5] The term "long tail" refers to a long tail distribution curve, as shown in the chart below, recognizing that there is much interest and activity beyond the "short head" at the "hit end" of the curve. A major lesson of *The Long Tail* is that people want what they want, not what you sell, and what they want goes well beyond the hits.

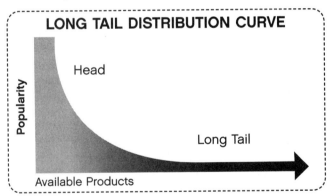

LONG TAIL DISTRIBUTION CURVE

Head

Long Tail

Popularity

Available Products

As we move down the tail we find the more narrow, eclectic, niche interests people have. People's interest in hits demonstrates what they have in common with others, while their interest in niches represents what makes them different. After all, a niche is, by definition, something that fewer people are interested in. The increased purchase activity that online retailers—unconstrained by shelf space—find on the long tail shows that we are not a homogeneous population, but a community of individuals.

[5]Chris Anderson, *The Long Tail* (New York: Hyperion Books, 2006), p. 23.

The week I am writing this, 24 million households are watching the number 1 rated television series, *CSI: Crime Scene Investigation*, which would be represented at the top of the head of a long tail curve. It's a safe assumption that people in virtually all those 21 million households watch other television programs in addition to *CSI: Crime Scene Investigation*. Are they all watching the same other programs? Obviously not, since every other program has fewer viewers than *CSI*. If we were able to map the total television viewing habits of all *CSI* viewers, we would see more and more differences between them as we moved down the long tail of the curve. Once we got down to shows with only tens of thousands of viewers, we would know that every *CSI* viewer watching that show was different from most every other *CSI* viewer, in at least that one interest. If we then stepped outside their television watching habits and looked at the other things they enjoy and do, we would see even more variation.

In other words, as we move down the curve, we see the interests and behaviors that make people unique. We see the spices in that last one-half of one percent that makes each person a one-of-a-kind individual. What defines us is not how we go with the masses towards what's popular, but how we behave in the narrow niches. Hit culture assumes everyone is the same; niche culture recognizes and values what makes each person unique.

One of the primary reasons that mass advertising's effectiveness continues to wane is that it is based on the idea that members of a mass media audience are similar. What the long tail concept shows is that our interest in hits or top sellers specifically doesn't define who we are; our interest in more narrow niches does. A powerful hit can actually mislead us about its audience's makeup, because it has the power to attract such a wide variety of people. There is no such thing as the typical *CSI* viewer. As Chris Anderson said in an interview I did with him for this book, "The fact that you and I both watch *CSI* is a relatively superficial connection between us. But if we were both into the latest in LEGO Robotics, that could make for quite a deep relationship between us. The loose ties are the mass ones, and the strong ties are the niche ones."

The long tail phenomenon does not describe just purchase or entertainment habits. Just about any characteristic people have follows a long tail distribution, meaning that there are items of mass interest ("hits"), followed by a large number of items of narrow, niche interest that sum cumulatively to large numbers. Many more people share an interest in blueberry muffins than share an interest in goose liver pâté, but if we were to look at a long-tailed distribution curve of a population's eating habits, we would see that the overall number of people who like specialized gourmet foods, such as goose liver pâté, is substantial. Most people engage in no regular exercise, and a relatively small number of people do Pilates. Yet, the number of people who partake in all different forms of exercise programs, cumulatively, is substantial; the number of people who partake in any one form may just be significantly less than the number of people in the population. If we want to understand exercise habits within a population, we would have to dig deeper than general, aggregated statistics and take a close look at the long tail. We can learn more interesting things about a person when we are alert to the niche behaviors that would help us understand his or her unique individuality.

Anderson quotes an article by Vin Crosbie from Corante,[6] discussing the myth that the media audience has only recently been fragmented:

> Each individual listener, viewer, or reader is, and has always been, a unique mix of generic interests and specific interests. Although many of these individuals might share some generic interests, such as the weather, most, if not all of them, each have very different specific interests. And each individual is a truly unique mix of generic and specific interests.

Your specific, non-generic interests are less popular; therefore, interest in them describes a way you are different. The narrower the niche in which you are interested, the more distinctive you are.

But it doesn't stop there. Anderson points out that a long tail curve is *fractal*, meaning that if you were to zoom in on a niche down

---

[6]rebuildingmedia.corante.com, November 15, 2005, Vin Crosbie, "A Perspective, The Myth of Audience Fragmentation."

on the tail, you would see that it also contains variety. Consider members of the narrowest niche you can think of...how about the members of the 6th Tennessee Dismounted Cavalry Regiment Civil War reenactment group? It would be easy to assume that each of these people was stamped from the same mold, but I'm certain that if we got to know them as individuals (a job I'm not volunteering for) we would see that each of them is unique in his own way.

Every one of us has our own portfolio of niches, which are the unique array of spices and flavors that reflect our specific personality and interests. The more you zoom in on the details, the more you can learn about other people. Our theme of individuality emerges again: We are defined not by how we are like other people, but by how we are different. A person's unique nature is more defined by his or her behavior down the long tail—you can learn more about a person's true, interesting character by their niche behavior than you can by the ways they blend into the crowd.

What does this tell us about creating We encounters?

In this section, we have been discussing the encounter-building element of uniqueness. We have focused on how a customer will more likely perceive an interaction as an encounter if he feels that the interaction has been created just for him. If you focus on the generic, broad-based characteristics representing things this customer has in common with many other people, such as "wears baggy jeans," "bleached hair," or "twenty-something," the interaction will not feel custom made. In fact, the person may sense that you are generalizing about him. If, on the other hand, you can recognize the more narrow niches that define this person—their interests and behaviors down the long tail of the curve—it will be easier to create an encounter in which the customer feels irreplaceable. If you can identify and speak with someone about his most unique characteristics, you will have a better chance of engaging with him. He will feel that the conversation is about him, not just about you or your product.

Moreover, as you discover the characteristics that make your customer most distinctive and inimitable, you will know your customer well enough to collaborate with him to fulfill his niche interests.

If your competitor only sees this customer in terms of broad, general, head-of-the-curve characteristics, your personalized interactions will seem much more relevant. For example, imagine you are selling cars, and a 22-year-old young man walks in, and, by his rough appearance, your first reaction is that his first interest in a car is speed. You engage him in a conversation and learn that this customer isn't what he seems; despite his tough exterior, he actually has a lot of anxiety about driving fast, due to a car accident when he was 19. What if your competitor gets misled by his appearance and tries to sell him the sportiest car in the showroom?

Additionally, the narrower and more specific your customer's need, the harder it will be for him to fulfill. After all, in a relatively efficient marketplace, solutions to his needs should be scarce, because there are very few people who share them. However, if you collaborate with your customer by getting to know him and working with him to discover what he wants, you will best be able to fulfill his needs. Relative to those who sell to his more generic characteristics, you will have added significant value.

We Encounters Are Long Tail Filters

Anderson calls catering to the long tail needs "filtering." He cites many illustrative examples from the world of online commerce, such as Google's search capabilities and the Netflix personalized recommendations described earlier. Good filtering helps a person find what he wants down the long tail, where the term "collaborative filtering" has also been used in recent years to describe computer-based models that predict a person's interests through use of algorithms applied to that person's characteristics and behaviors.

Although computers can be very powerful filters, collaborative filtering is at the essence of employing uniqueness in a We encounter. If, as the car salesperson from the example above, you employ your knowledge of the customer to help him fulfill his hard-to-find, down-the-tail, niche needs, you will be providing very valuable filtering. This will increase your customer's feeling that you are recognizing his distinct individuality, and you will have gone a long way to creating a relationship-building encounter.

Anderson describes that there is a low "signal to noise ratio" as you move down the long tail. This refers to the phenomenon we have mentioned that on the long tail there are more things you don't want ("noise") than things you want ("signal"); this is inherent since only relatively small numbers of people are interested in each item on the long tail. For example, if you were to go into a hardware store looking for a top-selling product, it might be on a display at the front of the store. If, however, you are trying to address a very specialized problem, virtually every product in that store would be like unwanted noise to you, and you would need help filtering through the inventory to find exactly what you need. A We encounter is a very productive way to help a customer filter through the noise and find exactly what he wants. Let's explore how.

The first element of an encounter we have discussed in this book, a moment with presence, creates the setting for collaborating with your customer. Once you are both in the moment with each other, it is possible to engage in a productive conversation, which is the second element of an encounter. This conversation, conducted with genuine dialogue, enables you and your customer to discover more about each other. You discover the details of his unique interests and needs, which represent the third element of an encounter, and, concurrently, you see what he doesn't want or need. You see opportunities to filter the noise, and you can now lead him to choices that are most relevant to him. As the conversation unfolds and you begin filtering the noise, he begins to see the distinct way that you can work with him to meet his individual interests and needs.

The more niche your customer's need is, i.e., the farther down the long tail this particular interest lies, the more valuable a We encounter becomes. If a customer walks into a Borders book store and wants the top-selling Dean Koontz novel, a mere transaction might be sufficient. However, if that customer wants something more obscure, the more important it will be to engage in a true encounter to help that customer filter the noise and find something that fulfills his interest.

In my interview with Chris Anderson, he describes how filtering for customers can actually help them discover things they didn't realize they wanted; he says that long tail economics "reveals the diversity that's there all along, and also stimulates diversity by opening people's eyes to variety and choice." When we help customers filter through the noise of near-infinite variety to find the specific things they really want, whether it is with an automated system or a rich, dialogue-laden, personal We encounter, we actually help them discover new interests they may not have previously realized.

The Long Tail is a powerful recognition of what really makes this economy a true "New Economy." As Anderson writes, "A Long Tail is just culture unfiltered by economic scarcity." The long tail concept recognizes that we are each truly unique, exceptional people, despite how much the forces of mass marketing, mass retailing, and mass manufacturing try to obscure that fact. Getting to know your customer and recognizing her "uniquenesses," niche interests, and niche behaviors—what's going on "down the tail"—is a major step for creating We.

"We Are Now Allowed"

To see someone as a full human being, even in a business context, look for the fine details of her character beyond those related to business. You can gain important insights into your customer by understanding her life beyond the matter at hand.

Stuart Hershkowitz, managing director of the private banking division of Bank of Jerusalem, competes against a number of large Israeli banks, most of which are not known for creating warm, cozy customer relationships. Stuart found a valuable competitive edge by focusing on a relationship-building strategy.

Stuart says that his most important relationship-building encounters include conversations that have nothing to do with banking. "I had a situation last week with people I haven't seen in thirty years. They came in to talk to me about a mortgage. We ended up not talking about the mortgage at all. We talked about everything in life. If I talk to someone only about a mortgage, I'll miss who he is. He's a lot more multi-dimensional than his mortgage. I always think '*Talk* to them! Try to find out who they are.' When I talk to someone, I see he's a person." Stuart is looking for the "spices" and details that define the

> It is accepted and expected to go beyond the strict bounds of business to create meaningful business relationships.

person that have nothing to do with his banking issues.

There are, of course, boundaries that limit the personal issues you can discuss with a customer. However, in general, we live in a day and age where it is more acceptable to bring our full selves, personal issues and all, into business situations.

A hotel salesperson articulated this beautifully in a workshop I conducted recently. We were discussing how to have meaningful encounters with customers and had arrived at a section of the workshop that focused on getting beyond the facade of business roles ("salesperson" and "customer") to see each other as unique, special people. She commented, "We are now allowed to talk about things beyond business, to ask about our customers' personal lives, so we can get to know them as people." Her belief—which I share—is that we have arrived at a point in time where genuine human encounter in business is more valued than it has been since the age of mass manufacturing and mass communication started. It is accepted and expected to go beyond the strict bounds of business to create meaningful business relationships. If the way you manage your encounters encourages your customer to share personal characteristics, you will be able to learn things about him or her that will help you understand this customer as a full human being.

We can best relate to customers as co-subjects, as partners in We, if we think of them not as abstractions, or manifestations of demographic generalities, but as complete, distinctive human beings. We may not know a customer as well as we know our siblings, but we recognize and appreciate that they are every bit as human as our kin. Each of them has a uniqueness that is there to be uncovered.

> One of the best ways to show a customer that you are diffferent is to show interest in what makes him different.

Additionally, if you believe in the full humanity of your customer, your customer will more likely relate to you in a truly human way. When a person is treated as an exceptional, special individual by another, he is more likely to see that other as an exceptional, unique person. This is a statement of a common observation in our personal lives; we need look no further than our closest friendships to understand this. All we must do is apply it to our business lives.

Stuart Hershkowitz describes it this way: "If a guy comes in and says 'What are your conditions for a mortgage?' and we just say, 'Fifteen years at blah blah interest rate,' he'll get up, turn around, and go to the next bank. He will try to see who's cheaper. Or he'll say, 'I didn't really get a feeling that anyone wants to talk to me; they were professional and that's it.'" One of the best ways to show a customer that you are different is to show interest in what makes him different.

And, of course, this means that it is not only appropriate to seek to know a customer as a real person, it is important for the person who is selling something to reveal his or her humanity. Salespeople playing the role of salespeople is out. Salespeople being themselves is in.

Here is a recap of a few steps I think are useful to creating a We encounter where each of you is there as a full, unique human being:

1) "Spot the spices." Our predisposition is to define someone by what makes him like other people, and not by what makes him unique. Try doing the opposite. Look for the things that make a person unique, their "long tail" niche interests and behaviors. As we've said, it is the seemingly small things that define us, the spices and flavors that make us interesting. Defining people by what makes them like others is lazy. Defining a person by what makes him unique is enriching.

2) **Don't limit your observations about a person to the matter at hand.** A person's uniqueness extends well beyond the ways she uses your product or service. If you are curious and willing to learn about your customer, well beyond the direct features that relate to your product, you will learn things that help you engage with that customer.

3) **Always believe that you are unique.** Challenge yourself to answer this question in every encounter: *Am I the only person in the world who could be doing this, in this same way, right now, or could someone substitute for me and have it be exactly the same?* Sure, one of your colleagues may be able to stand in for you on the basic "job task" taking place in the encounter. But, have you approached the encounter with your own genuine, full, unique humanity? Are you there as yourself, or as a representative of your job role? One of the easiest ways to bring out the uniqueness in someone else is to make it easier for them to see what makes you unique.

Seven Billion People, So Little Time

Clearly, you cannot interact with every person you have contact with as a unique person. The day is too short.

There is a little-known story about Martin Buber showing up very late for a speech. After the audience waited more than two hours for the eminent professor, he finally showed up with another man, for whom Buber requested a front row seat. At the end of the speech, before taking questions, Buber shook the man's hand, and the man left. Buber then apologized for being late and explained that the man was his cab driver and that they had been engaged in a very deep conversation. The lesson in this story is not that we shouldn't have rich encounters with cab drivers, but that we can only afford to invest time in a limited number of people. By focusing on the cab driver, Professor Buber chose to favor the encounter with him at the expense of the audience for the speech. Whether that was the right choice is beside the point; the point is that there is a choice. Likewise,

> To create productive, profitable, and sustainable We relationships, we have to pursue fewer high-quality relationships at the expense of many superficial acquaintances. You can't be friends with everyone.

you can't afford to invest in learning the exceptional features of every person you meet, and then interacting with all of them based on what you learn. You won't be able to get anything done.

To create productive, profitable, and sustainable We relationships, we have to pursue fewer high-quality relationships at the expense of many superficial acquaintances. Life requires us to be selective about the relationships we pursue, and this process starts from the moment we meet a new person. The sad but true fact is that early in a relationship you must determine if this person or organization warrants your relationship investment. You can't be friends with everyone.

You can't get to know all seven billion people on the planet, so you might as well start being selective now.

NOTICE>> As you interact with people, pay attention to the spices— the small details that make this person special. Notice how these details give you a more complete picture of the person.

Perspective

I recently ran an executive retreat for a manufacturing company that sells its products through major retailers throughout the U.S. The president of the company and I believed that his team did not have a clear picture of what it was like, from the customer's perspective, to do business with the company. To address this, we organized the company's top fifty executives into teams, and, three weeks before the retreat, we assigned each team one of the company's products. The teams were asked to visit retail outlets and buy the product they were assigned. After that, they were to assemble the products, use the products, call customer service, and do many other things a normal customer might have to do.

At the retreat we asked each team to make a short presentation to share their experience as a customer of the company. As the teams filed up to the front of the room and described what happened, a pattern quickly emerged. Group after group described how cumbersome the customer experience was—confusing packaging, poorly written assembly manuals, difficult assembly, long waits on the phone for customer service, etc. They looked shell-shocked, bewildered, and amazed. Comments such as "I can't believe we do this to our customers," "I had no idea," "It's a wonder anyone buys from us" filled the room.

Many companies would have a similar experience if they tried this exercise.

One of the most difficult things for humans to do is to see things from the perspective of other people. Think of the times you and someone else completely disagreed, yet you each held your beliefs with strong conviction. I'm sure you are both smart and reasonable people; why didn't you see eye to eye?

Our different life experiences, our different needs, and our different ways of thinking create biases that fuel disagreement. You loved that movie? I couldn't stand it. You hated that novel? It was one of my favorites. Bias can be a key driver of miscommunication.

Think how likely it is that you and one of your customers could see things differently. Your businesses have different needs and goals and face different issues. You think about your product all day long (and sometimes during the night), and they think about your product only a fraction of the time. They may see you as only one of many interchangeable suppliers, whereas you understand how subtle differences between you and your competitors translate to meaningful strengths and weaknesses.

One of the most critical aspects of a successful We relationship is the ability to bridge this chasm of perspective. You, of course, would like your customer to see things from your perspective. This, of course, can't happen unless you begin to see things from your customer's perspective.

The image that comes to my mind is of an "out of body experience," where you are able to leave your own perspectives and biases to the side and get a really clear view of what you, your product, and the relationship between you and your customer look like from the customer's point of view.

Strip away everything you know about your product and your company. (Yes—it's difficult!) What would you *really* look like to someone who has just made your acquaintance? What would you look like to someone who has known you for a while? Do you feel confident in the answers?

People in organizations create stories—reinforced by the conversations they have with each other—about what customers think is important, about how customers view the organization, about how well they are able to meet customers' needs. Numerous market research professionals have remarked to me—and my own experience has confirmed this—that there is often a large gap between what companies believe their customers think and what the customers *actually* think. It is difficult for us to realize just how much fog our own position and perspective create when it comes to understanding what we look like from where the customer is standing.

Not surprisingly, it is often the senior executives who have the most inaccurate view of customer perspectives. Not only do many senior executives have little contact with actual customers, they are often shielded from the kinds of problems that customers encounter daily. Years ago, I worked with a hotel company whose CEO felt indignant when he heard customer complaints. "We don't treat people that way," he would say. But the fact was that he had no idea how his company treated people, because his personal experience in his company's hotels lacked any resemblance to what a typical guest would receive. Hotels knew in advance that he was coming, and they did everything to prepare for a perfect stay. During his stay, the hotel took every precaution to avoid problems, in order to show him how well-run this particular hotel was. Once, when he was in a hotel with his family, a hotel employee was stationed in the room across the hall, looking continuously through the view hole in the door, waiting for a family member to emerge. Once the family's door would open, the employee would run to the phone and call down to the front desk. "They're coming!" No wonder he found complaints by real customers perplexing.

If I want to understand what the world looks like to you, from where you are standing, I have to step out of my experience and into yours. My story must retreat into the background so I can hear yours. I have to pause and move into inquiry. I have to be curious about you, and the way you see the world.

> **TRY THIS>>** **Look for ways to see your company or organization from the customer's perspective. Try out your customer experience. If you have retail locations where you will not be recognized, or call centers where your voice is not familiar, pose as a customer to see what your organization looks like from that vantage point. If you will be recognized, ask someone else to visit or call your company and have her describe the experience in detail. If your business takes orders and ships product, go ahead and place an order, receive the product, use it, break it, fix it—and see what the experience is like.**

Sensitivity—Understand What Your Customer Feels and Thinks

SCENARIO 1: I fly on a major airline. It is a perfect, frictionless travel experience. I check in with no hassle, there is no wait at security. The airline has assigned a convenient gate. The seat next to me is open, leaving me more room. We leave on time and fly through clear skies to our destination, arriving at the gate 15 minutes early.

My experience walking off the plane: The flight attendant and pilot are standing by the cockpit door saying, "Thank you. Hope you enjoyed your flight."

SCENARIO 2: I fly on a major airline. It is a nightmare travel experience. The check-in line is in gridlock, since the airline's computer system is down. After a long wait at the counter I confront a serious bottleneck at security, where I am subjected to a random search of my bags and person. After these delays, I am forced to run to a gate at the end of the concourse, where I board the plane with only minutes to spare. There is no room left in the overhead compartments, so the flight attendant insists on checking my bag. I am wedged into a middle seat between a rotund man with overactive sweat glands and a mother with a crying baby. We fly through turbulent air and are forced to circle the airport in bad weather as we wait for clearance to land, arriving an hour and a half late.

My experience walking off the plane: The flight attendant and pilot are standing by the cockpit door saying, "Thank you. Hope you enjoyed your flight."

All I can think: This airline is completely insensitive to me and my experience as their customer.

Do you have a clear sense of how things are going for your customer? Is your radar honed to pick up signals—whether faint or blaring—that tell you when things go right or wrong in your relationship?

> **Be alert to your own alertness: What is the other person feeling, and what is my data for that?**

Understanding a customer as a unique person with unique situations is not a static thing. People change continually, situations change regularly. To interact with your customer as a unique person, you must stay in tune with him and be sensitive to what happens to him, especially in relation to your organization. Dr. Jay Ferraro recommends that we "always ask ourselves the right questions: What is the other person feeling, and what is my data for that?" Be alert to your own alertness of your customer's situation.

If you are creating encounters with customers—being in the moment with them, creating rich conversations with them, and interacting with them as unique, authentic people in unique, authentic interactions—you won't have to try hard to be sensitive to your customers in this way. You will know. Encounters not only build relationships, they help people understand each other in ways that transactions never can.

THE ENCOUNTER'S AFTERGLOW: THE FEELING OF "WITH"

You have created an encounter with a customer.

You are both present and fully engaged in the moment.

Your conversation is rich in dialogue.

You both recognize each other as unique human beings, creating a fresh moment that has never happened before.

It feels as if you have done something *with* each other.

Transactions don't feel this way. In a transaction the other person may do something *for* you, or they may even do something *to* you.

Encounters are mutual, and inherently collaborative. This feeling of "with" is the magic ingredient that makes it possible for a single encounter to be a building block of a mutual, collaborative We relationship. It creates an inkling that you can work together, a foreshadowing of the relationship you will have if you create more encounters like this one.

3

FROM ENCOUNTER TO RELATIONSHIP: THE ONGOING CONVERSATION

A RELATIONSHIP FORMS FROM A CONTINUITY OF ENCOUNTERS

My wife, Arna, tells me about her experience buying glasses for our son Levi a few months previously, before he left for a semester of study overseas: "The salesperson at Lenscrafters, Trish, was amazing. We were looking at different frames, and I noticed that she was remembering little things about Levi, what he liked, what he didn't like, what he said he'd be doing on his trip. We decided to go have lunch and think about the options, and when we came back Trish remembered all those things. We picked up right where we'd left off and bought the glasses. Then, we came back a week later to buy Levi prescription sunglasses. She remembered all about what kind of frames he liked, and she immediately recommended the right sunglasses for him. Then, I went back to Lenscrafters a month later, and as soon as she saw me she said, "How's school going for Levi?"

As powerful as it is, a single encounter only hints at the power of human interaction. The true magic of human encounter occurs when encounters connect, forming themselves into human relationships.

Arna's first interaction with Trish at Lenscrafters was a good encounter. Trish was totally present, she engaged my wife and son in a good dialogue, and she recognized my son's uniqueness and related to him based on what she learned about him. But what caught Arna's attention, and distinguished Trish from other retail salespeople, was the way she connected the series of encounters together. Each encounter was a gem, but from them all taken together Trish created a stunning piece of jewelry.

Trish was alert and in the moment, so she noticed things about Levi and remembered them. Her reference to previous conversations about Levi demonstrated that she was interacting with him as a distinct person, not just another customer. This also supported a feeling of conversation; she had obviously been listening. In addition, Trish revealed a few things about herself in their first meeting, which not only helped Arna see her as a unique person, but helped Arna also connect their two meetings. Trish wasn't just another salesperson. She was Trish.

A We relationship builds as a series of We encounters connect to each other, forming a continuity. Each encounter may be valuable in and of itself, but as these encounters connect and reference each other, a greater value is formed—a relationship.

A Continuity of Encounters

Picture a jeweler sitting down to work, a cluster of beautiful pearls on his table. As he prepares to work, the light glistening off the individual pearls catches the eye. But as the jeweler begins to string the pearls, the beauty of the individual pearls is not what is noticeable anymore. It is the strand of pearls, one next to the other. This connection of individual gems, as a grouping, far surpasses the beauty and value of the individual pearls.

As a series of moments string together, your customer can perceive something much greater than the sum of all individual encounters. The series itself begins to take on a character, a personality that helps your customer form feelings about you, your organization, and/or your product. Like the necklace whose beauty outweighs the sum of the individual pearls on its strand, the series itself becomes the main thing of beauty.

MEMORY IS THE CONNECTION BETWEEN ENCOUNTERS

"A RELATIONSHIP IS, ESSENTIALLY, A SERIES OF MEMORIES."
— NEUROPSYCHOLOGIST DR. MICHAEL GELBORT

What bonds one encounter to another? What helps link them together to form a relationship?

For encounters to form a continuity, it is necessary for the participants in those encounters to connect and carry with them memories from one encounter to the next.

> **Your challenge is not only to create memory for yourself, but to be memorable.**

If you and your customer carry clear, palpable, meaningful memories out of one encounter, and those memories remain clear, palpable, and meaningful at the time of your next meeting, there is a high likelihood that these two encounters will connect to each other.

What we are talking about is as simple and yet elusive as this: How do you and your customer come out of one encounter with memories so clear and compelling that you both remember and can use that memory to enhance your next encounter?

Note carefully that we are talking about two memories: yours and your customer's. Your challenge is not only to create a memory for yourself, but also to be memorable. You must help your customer create a palpable memory of you and the encounter.

What Makes a Memory Palpable?

Not surprisingly, people are more likely to remember things that are of significance to them.

Dr. Michael Gelbort is a clinical neuropsychologist in Joliet, Illinois. He is an expert in memory, and much of his practice focuses on memory disorders caused by physical trauma. Dr. Gelbort explains: "What makes memory most likely to occur is if there's some sort of 'emotional loading,' and an emotional meaning to what the person encounters or experiences. When you work with people with memory disturbance, or people who are losing their memory or not forming memories very well, you can start seeing the patterns. People rarely remember things that have little interest or little importance to them. Things that have some sort of significance are more likely to be encoded, stored, and then consolidated so that they're available later on."

As all good teachers know, people are more likely to remember a concept if it has a number of different connections to various parts of their life. "Memories that are most durable are things that have a variety of hooks or a variety of meanings for the person," says Dr. Gelbort. "It's much easier to hang on to random memories if they fit into a whole schema, a whole organizational framework. Then, all of a sudden, things link together, and it's much easier to remember the whole picture."

Another aspect of this concept is that people also tend to remember things when they receive "multi-modal" inputs, i.e., if they hear something, see it, touch, smell, and/or hold it, they will be much more likely to create a palpable memory than if they come into contact with it in only one way. "The more different ways you experience something at the same time," continues Dr. Gelbort, "the more different hooks there are in your memory, the more ways there are to go back and find it when you search your memory banks. The way our memories work is that the more different connections we have, the more meaning it carries and the more ways there are to get back into that memory."

People also tend to have different styles for remembering things. For example, some people are visual learners, who tend to create clear memories of things they see. Others are more likely to retain sounds, words, or concepts. Understanding your style—or your customer's memory style—can be very helpful in creating memories of encounters.

In each encounter you or your organization has with customers, you need to form memories that you can use in subsequent encounters. You have to determine what is worth remembering, and then find a way to remember it.

Whether that memory is stored in one person's brain or in a CRM database so it can be shared by people throughout your company, the principles are the same. Keep track of information you learn that can create a bridge to a successful future encounter.

Determining What to Remember

It is impossible to remember all details of an encounter. And, even if you could remember all those details, you wouldn't want to. Many of them would not be necessary in future encounters with this customer.

The first challenge is to identify what is worth remembering, so you can focus on those most important things. This is another opportunity to use a technique we explored earlier: Bring the future

> **Think ahead: "What, from this meeting, will I want to know in our next encounter?"**

forward into the present moment. Think ahead to the next encounter, and ask yourself, "What, from this meeting, will I want to know in our next encounter?" Imagine a rich conversation in your next meeting. Envision the kinds of things from this meeting that you will want to weave into that conversation. Then, focus your memory formation on those things.

Remembering

Conscious awareness of what you want to remember will automatically help you remember those things better. Just by determining what you want to remember, you will help yourself remember.

In addition to that, there are a number of memory strategies that you can employ to help you bring strong memories with you out of an encounter. As we discussed previously, people are more likely to remember things if they interact with them in multiple, "multi-modal" ways. For example, if you hear someone's name, you will be more likely to remember it if you repeat it. If you are introduced to Jean, say, "Hi, Jean. How are you?" We also discussed how connections to other parts of your life can help you remember concepts and events. I find that I can more easily remember a situation if I consciously think of similar situations I've been in before.

Note taking can aid memory, even if you never refer to the notes. Dr. Gelbort describes how this works in his practice: "A memory strategy that we teach people with memory disturbance is to write notes. I tell my patients that if they're writing short notes to themselves about things to do, after two or three months, most of them don't need to write the notes. Just the simple act of writing the note causes the brain to make its own 'internal note.'"

I specifically orient my note-taking in a business meeting around things that I think I will want to refer to in a future encounter with this customer. These items become the main framework of my notes, and I write down other things in the margins or at a separate place on the notes. You may find it easier to make notes that track the conversation chronologically, and block off a special part of the note paper to record things you want to remember. In any case, you can help your memory by writing down the things that you have determined are important to remember.

Sometimes you don't even need a pen and pencil to write the note. Dr. Gelbort encourages people, if they don't have an opportunity to write, to take their finger and form the letters. "You're doing something tactile; you're encoding it into another portion of your brain. You've got a memory for touch, just as you have a memory for auditory information and for visual information." This is a useful technique if you are walking with a customer or eating in a restaurant and want to increase the likelihood that you will remember something.

Another strategy to help you remember is to immediately review the encounter directly after it happens.

> A friend described for me how she learned to remember history lessons when she was in high school: "Mr. Pasquini always told us that if we would review what we learned right after we left the classroom we wouldn't have to study as hard for the tests. 'Take a moment when you leave, even if it's while you're walking to your next class, and think about what we've talked about. You'll be surprised how much more you'll remember.'"

A meeting doesn't have to end at the end of the meeting. Resist the temptation to grab your phone and check for messages as soon as you leave a meeting. Don't be too eager to get out of the moment. Pause after the encounter and review what happened. You will be surprised how much more you will remember of what went on.

Dr. Gelbort also explains that sleep consolidates memory. "It's a real mistake for students not to study the night before a test. Sleep does for memories what the refrigerator does for Jell-O. It solidifies it." By thinking about a customer meeting the day or night before, you will have better access to memories in the next day's encounter.

These techniques can help you, even if you are concerned that your memory isn't very strong. As Dr. Gelbort says, "Although there are lots of little things you can do to remember things better, you're not actually improving your memory. You're just recognizing the way it works, and then using it in consonance with the way it works."

Company-wide Memory

> Customer Relationship Management Systems should be called Customer Memory Systems.

Essentially, the same memory principles should apply when your entire company has a need to remember things about a customer. Since the early 1990s, companies have spent billions on customer relationship management database systems. My experience, as a consultant, is that most companies are ill-equipped, regardless of the sophistication of their computer-based applications, to remember the *right* things about their customers. Their systems are often not designed to track the things that make a customer unique. Front-line employees are not adequately trained, or given incentives to record the unique features of customers, or to retrieve and use information another employee has recorded in a previous encounter. The key to these systems is to use them to support memory, so that subsequent encounters can be better connected with previous encounters.

It is actually unfortunate that these systems are called Customer Relationship Management Systems, because people then assume that the management of customer relationships can be delegated to a computer. We would be much better served if we called them Customer Memory Support Systems.

> **NOTICE>>** Think of companies you do business with, from small retail stores to mega-corporations. How well do they remember things about you?

> **HOW DO YOU COMPARE>>** How well does your organization remember things about its customers? And, if one person creates a memory about a customer, can

the information be easily transferred to another person in order to be remembered in a future encounter?

TRY THIS>> In your next encounter, consciously think, "What will I want to remember in our next meeting?" If it is appropriate, write those things into your notes during the encounter. If it is not appropriate to write, make mental notes. Then, in your subsequent meeting with this customer, refer back to those things and be aware of how they tie the two encounters together.

Your Customer's Memory— How to Make an Encounter Memorable

"IF YOU UNDERSTAND HOW SOMEONE THINKS AND REMEMBERS THINGS, BEING MEMORABLE IS LIKE PLANTING A SEED YOU CAN HARVEST LATER."—NEUROPSYCHOLOGIST DR. MICHAEL GELBORT

You also have the responsibility of making it easier for your customers to create palpable memories about their encounters with you. In other words, you want your encounters to be memorable.

The same principles that we discussed to support your own memory formation can make you and your encounters more memorable. For example, give people multiple hooks upon which to create a memory. Combine visual representation with a verbal description. In seminars and workshops I always ensure that participants speak and write, not only because they will enjoy the process more, but because they will be much more likely to retain what they learn.

This is another compelling reason to engage people in dialogue. In addition to all the reasons we have discussed that make dialogue a critical part of encounters, if people are engaged in a dialogue, as opposed to just listening to something, they will be able to form clearer, stronger, and more palpable memories.

Since we were children we've known that stories are more memorable than lists of facts. Any time you can wrap information you want to communicate in a story, that information will be more memorable. Doug Stevenson, the storytelling expert we met earlier, described a situation to me that has happened to him many times. He meets someone who says they heard him give a speech a few years previously. This person doesn't remember Doug's name, and may not even remember the subject of the speech, but they remember one of Doug's stories with great clarity.

Metaphors, if chosen carefully, work in the same way. For example, I wanted a client to focus on the opportunity cost of not proceeding with a certain strategy. I told her that it was like the floor of her office was covered with money and we weren't bending down to pick it up. This picture was so clear that it became an ongoing metaphor in our conversations as the project progressed. ("We picked up some more cash off the floor today!")

In developing a brand strategy for another client, we focused on the way they help their customers find the best course of action for completing projects. In our discussions, I used a number of metaphors related to navigating a ship. It helped members of the client team retain the concepts from one meeting to the next.

Keying in on the customer's interests is a relatively easy way to help her form palpable memories; we know that people will remember something better if it is emotionally relevant to them, personally. For example, if you were selling a car to someone and you learned that the person was concerned about appearing too ostentatious by having a fancy car, you could emphasize models and colors that were more understated. The customer would be more likely to remember what you said because these are features that concern her. In a business-to-business setting, I have often referred to the client's overall business goals in conversations, beyond the specific scope of our work together, because I know that the client spends a lot of time thinking about these goals. If I focus on the things that are most important to my customer, she will be more likely to remember the conversation with me.

When you combine the idea of story with personal relevance, you can find a way to make an encounter more memorable for a customer. Don't just tell someone a list of points. If you can, through dialogue, engage them in a story that is of special interest to them. We discussed examples of this earlier. For instance, I described how I discussed an employee marketing program with an executive. Instead of just describing the program, we engaged in a discussion of scenarios where, in the future, his employees were either supporting or not supporting the company's new brand strategy. Not only did this story, in which he was actively engaged and which actively involved him, make our encounter more relevant, it also helped him create a better memory of our meeting.

Additionally, people will remember things better if you give them a context for learning something. Often people explain things in a business meeting to people who don't have the context or framework to understand what they are hearing. As a neuropsychologist, Michael Gelbort is often called on to be an expert witness. "For example, I often see people try to explain things to a jury that the jury is not equipped to understand. I like to give people a way to think about something first, and then when I explain it, they are ready to hear it. If I first describe what happens with certain brain injuries, or how they are caused, then it will be easier for me to help the jury understand and remember things in the way I want them to. It's the pre-teaching notion. You teach them how to think about it, and then you give them the thing to think about. I think what a lot of people do is oftentimes just give you the thing to think about, and you don't know how to think about it."

As with dialogue and conversation, uniqueness not only makes for good encounters, it makes for good memories. When you create a unique, one-of-a-kind encounter, it will inherently be more memorable. It will not be lost in your customer's brain among similar memories.

I have had good results by sharing things about my personal life with clients to help them see me as unique. This clearly can't work in every business situation, but, if appropriate, it is a great way to make yourself memorable. For example, I play in a band with my eighteen-year old son, and clients often ask me about the band once they have heard about it. My musical avocation isn't a key part of the Yastrow Marketing brand strategy, but it seems to help people form more lasting memories about me.

Determine What You Want Your Customer to Remember

> **Think ahead: What do you want your customer to remember in your next encounter?**

In determining what you should remember, I suggested earlier that you bring the future forward and think ahead to your next encounter, imagining what you will want to remember at that time. Similarly, you can think ahead to your next meeting and imagine what you will want your customer to remember, in order to connect that encounter to your previous encounters.

When you think ahead to what you will want your customer to remember in the future, a number of things will become clear. It will help you focus the current conversation on those things. It will give you a foundation for follow-up conversations.

> **NOTICE>>** How frequently do people who sell to you make it easy to remember things about them? What do they do to help you remember these things?

> **HOW DO YOU COMPARE>>** How easy do you and your organization make it for your customers to remember you? What could you do better?

> **TRY THIS>>** In your next customer encounter, think forward. What do you most want your customer to remember about you, and about the encounter?

THE RHYTHM OF ENCOUNTER—BUILDING MOMENTUM IN YOUR RELATIONSHIP

Relationships Take (a Sense of) Time

A relationship with a customer begins. It is off to a good start. The outlook is promising. But a successful, productive, long-term relationship is not a foregone conclusion.

There are many courses that this relationship can take. It may bloom into something special, something that will be meaningful to both you and your customer. Or, like most nascent relationships, it can wither before its time.

> One of the most important decisions you can make about your new relationship is "when."

The factors that play a role in these different outcomes are many. One of the most critical is the pace of encounters, the actual rhythm that you and your customer feel as a series of encounters unfolds.

Think for a moment of a room full of percussionists. Virtuosos assembled in a room, sitting with a variety of drums, some played with sticks, some with hands. Now think of the wide range of rhythms they could choose to play. They could play a rhythm of aggressive pulses, or they could, instead, create a sweet, sparse drizzle of ethereal sounds punctuated by silence. The rhythm could start softly and build to a climax, or it could start strong and ebb and flow through a cycle of dynamic changes. The choices available to these percussionists are innumerable. Consider for a moment how much the choices they make will define the character of their music.

Now think of the choices you have as a customer relationship begins to emerge. In your excitement to create a strong relationship, you might be tempted to create a rapid-fire series of encounters, in order to ensure that your new customer doesn't forget about you or lose you in the competing rhythms of his life. Or, maybe you are very busy, and you make the choice (by default) to engage in only a limited number of encounters in support of this new relationship.

The point is as simple as this: The actual rhythm of encounters is critical to the success of your new relationship, and you have significant control of this rhythm. One of the most important decisions you can make about your new relationship is "when."

This decision is all about crafting the pace of your relationship. It is about creating a rhythm of interaction between you and your customer, and, as with the percussionists, rhythm is a very effective communicator.

There are many aspects of this rhythm over which you have only limited control. Your customer is not always available to have an encounter with you. You may live and work far from each other, creating a real obstacle that influences the pace of encounters.

Do not view these limitations as total constraints. They set boundaries, but, within those boundaries, you have a great deal of control. Your challenge is to compose a cadence of encounters that, within the realities of your situation, optimally supports the growth of your relationship. My observation is this: If a relationship fails to grow past inception due to a problem with the rhythm of encounters, it is most often due not to logistical constraints, but due to neglect of factors within one's control.

Manage the "when." Don't let it manage you.

The Key to "When"

When it comes to "when," there is a danger in both directions. It is possible to have too few encounters, and it is possible to have too many.

It is important to have enough encounters. A pre-school teacher gave me a relevant example that helps us understand this. "Families these days are inevitably stretched for time. Opportunities to spend time with the kids are limited, so parents work to compensate for this by focusing on 'quality time.' As I see it, quality itself rarely makes up for a lack of quantity. Yes, kids need the full quality attention of their parents, but they also need to have enough different occasions to be with their parents."

It's easy to translate this example of focusing on quality time to customer relationships. You plan for the next big meeting with a customer. If you're in a professional services business, this might be a big presentation summarizing work you've done. If you run a restaurant, it may be a private party your valued customer holds at your place every few months. Whatever the nature of your business, these major moments need a lot of your attention, and they get that attention. But can your relationship thrive solely on "quality time?" Would a little more quantity help fuel your relationship? Can you create additional encounters between the major moments to enhance the rhythm of the relationship?

And, clearly, it is easy to have too many interactions with customers. Every time I make the effort to clean my email inbox, I am amazed at the frequency of contact some sellers have programmed

> **If you overload customers with too many contacts, they will hit delete in their mental mailboxes.**

into their email marketing programs. Two or three emails per week may be sitting in my inbox, unread, from one company. If you overload customers with too many contacts, they will feel bothered by you, and they will not value your communications. They will hit delete in their mental mailboxes. Like the waiter who stops by the table too frequently, interrupting your dinner conversation, too many contacts can turn your best intentions into pestering. The advertising mindset has taught us that more frequency is always better, but this is based on a transactional type of communication that is not very effective at getting the attention of customers. If you are connecting with customers in encounters, more is not always better.

Following are some ideas for gauging the appropriate number of encounters in a relationship.

Are You Creating Enough Encounters to Develop Adequate Memory?

Joe's first meeting with Midwest Bank went very well. They seemed extremely interested in learning more about his approach to software training, and he felt confident that he could make a sale to them at his next appointment. But it was three weeks before they could see him again, and five minutes into this second meeting it is obvious to Joe that he has to start over. He can tell that Diana, the head of operations, isn't sure if his first name is Jim or Joe. Bill, the office manager who has direct responsibility for computer training, has forgotten most of what they had discussed at the first meeting. Joe hoped to build on the first meeting, but his customers don't have memories that are clear enough to make that possible.

As discussed above, memory is the most primary connection between encounters. If your customer's memories are inadequate, you will not be able to create a series of encounters.

In this case, Joe's constraint was that he couldn't get on the bank's calendar for three weeks, which proved to be too long for his prospective clients to retain the concepts they had discussed in the initial meeting. Upon reflection, though, Joe realized that he could have done things to manage this situation by creating additional interactions with his customer.

- He could have written a short one-page note to Bill and Diana the day after the first meeting, summarizing what he heard them say and the solutions they discussed.

- Recognizing that they might not have read the note, he could have resent it via email the day prior to the second meeting, and left each of them a voicemail message suggesting that they take a quick look at the note, which summarizes the last meeting.

These two short, minor communications could have served as a bridge between the two meetings. Yes, Bill and Diana might have ignored Joe's email and voicemail messages, but he would have increased the odds that they would have remembered the content of the previous meeting. And even if they had only printed out his note, giving it a quick glance as they took it off the printer, there is still a chance he would have sparked their minds enough for them to remember more about the earlier conversation.

Pay attention as you speak with a customer, noticing how well he remembers your past encounters. If you see that he has forgotten things, from subtle details to major issues, you may want to plan some intermediary encounters to act as a bridge between more important meetings.

If you and your customer don't seem to be learning enough about each other to fuel the growth of your relationship, you may have to create additional encounters to address this issue. For example, if you find that you have a need to know more about a customer's business to see what makes them unique, ask to meet with additional people in the company, even those who aren't directly involved with your work. In most cases, customers appreciate that you are willing to learn things about them that don't directly benefit you. It says a lot.

You may notice that your customer doesn't understand well enough what makes you unique. In this case, you will have to engineer some encounters that can better communicate the nuances of your story. If it could be relevant, invite customers to your facility, and use that opportunity to engage them in a We encounter. If appropriate, ask your customer for feedback on your performance, or for advice on a business issue.

Are You Creating Too Many Encounters?

If your encounters with a customer are too frequent, the customer may begin to take you for granted and will not give adequate attention to the interactions he has with you. Your meetings will seem routine and uneventful.

Remember that it is the outdated advertising mindset that has taught us to think that having more contacts with a customer is always better. But it is wrong to use advertising frequency as a guide for determining the pace of We encounters. Customers don't notice most advertising, which is not surprising, considering that they are exposed to as many as 5,000 advertising and promotional messages a day. More is not always better.

✳

TOO FEW ENCOUNTERS	THE RIGHT NUMBER OF ENCOUNTERS	TOO MANY ENCOUNTERS
Your customers can't clearly remember the nuances of past encounters.	Your customers' memory of past encounters is strong enough.	Your customer takes your encounters for granted, devaluing them.
You and your customer don't know enough about each other.	You and your customer are able to learn what makes each other unique.	Your encounters seem routine.

Pay attention to the pace of encounters, and to the relationship that is forming, to determine if you are creating the right number of encounters. In the evolution of a We relationship, "when" is nearly as important as "what."

THE MIX OF MOMENTS—MILESTONES AND BRIDGES

Of course, a customer relationship includes the major moments that act as the building blocks of your relationship. But don't forget that blocks will never become buildings without mortar. The tiny, transitional encounters with your customer act as the mortar that cements your relationship.

Milestone Moments

As you plan the pace of encounters in your customer relationship—the "when"—it is natural to focus first on the major milestones. As you cultivate a new customer, the next milestone may be a major meeting to discuss a proposal. Or with a current customer, the next milestones may include interactions that are central to your relationship, such as product or service delivery, or the next time he visits your place of business.

> The tiny, transitional encounters with your customer act as the mortar that cements your relationship.

These milestones are the defining moments that reveal the course of your relationship. This is where the major changes in direction—for better or worse—happen. It makes sense to craft the pace of these major milestones first.

To do this, use the tools of marketing and brand planning described in chapter 5 of my book *Brand Harmony,* which I will re-view here.

These steps will be explained below, using an example of a software company planning the pace of milestone moments during a project with a customer.

What is the relationship's "picture of success?"
First, define the results you want to achieve with this relationship.

Where do you want this relationship to be in the future, and what benefits do you want you and your customer to be achieving from it at that time? If the relationship is new, or at a critical juncture, you may define the future of your planning horizon in terms of weeks or only a few months. For a more mature relationship, you may be thinking of a time period as long as a year or more. Describe to yourself a "picture of success" for this relationship by describing, in detail, what is happening at that future time period. How much business will you be doing together? What benefits are both of you deriving from the relationship?

As an example, consider a critical upcoming three-month period in the relationship between a software company, Delta Partners, and a client. Delta Partners' picture of success is the successful implementation of a new upgrade, with success defined as all the client's employees transitioning to the new version of the software during a two-day cutover period at the end of this three-month period.

What actions do you and your customer have to take?

Note that realizing your picture of success is highly dependent on actions taken by your customer. No matter what actions you take personally, the success of your We relationship requires that your customers do certain things. Now, define what it is you would like your customer to do to make your picture of success a reality. Think of all the things you want them to do in support of your relationship, from the small things like talking about you with their colleagues to the more obvious actions like purchasing, using, and reordering your product.

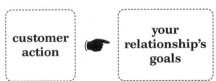

Delta Partners knows in detail what it has to do, but also recognizes that success is dependent on actions taken by people in the client organization. These actions include the scheduling of training classes, allowing Delta Partners access to the client's internal IT staff, installing new computer hardware, and gaining senior management approval for payments, among others. Delta Partners identifies 15 different people in the client organization who will have to take these actions in order for the project to succeed. Five of them are "official" members of the software upgrade project team; the other 10 are key managers throughout the organization whose departments will be substantially affected by the upgrade.

What do you want your customer to believe about the relationship?

One of the key principles of Brand Harmony is that customer action is driven by what a customer believes. This belief is your customer's brand impression.

What is the brand impression you want your customer to have of your relationship?

Therefore, you now must describe what your customer would have to believe about your relationship in order to take those actions. What we are describing is as simple, yet powerful, as this: What is the brand impression you want your customer to have of your *relationship*, not only of your product?

Delta Partners understands its client well and knows that it is not a foregone conclusion that all of these actions will happen. Yet, Delta Partners also knows that if these actions don't happen, and the upgrade does not proceed successfully, it is unlikely that the client will recognize their responsibility for the failure. Therefore, it is critical to help a number of people in the client organization understand how much their actions are tied to the project's success. It is time to define the desired brand impressions Delta Partners wants the client to have of this particular project.

The best way to do this is to define, in the client's own words, what

> **The encounters in your relationship create the story of your relationship.**

Delta Partners wants the client to be saying and thinking. For example, Delta Partners might determine that it needs its main contacts at the client company to think, "It is critical that I work to align internal resources in order to make this project a success," or, "I must ensure that people throughout our company cooperate fully with Delta Partners." The most important part of this step is that Delta Partners defines desired brand impressions in the client's own words. By writing in the first person, playing the role of the client, Delta Partners will define a much truer sense of what the clients should be thinking.

Your customers will form that brand impression of your relationship as a result of the cumulative encounters they have with you and your organization. The encounters in your relationship create the story of your relationship. You are now able to define the major moments that will become that story.

Identify the milestone moments that create the relationship's story

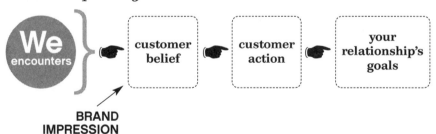

After defining what Delta Partners wants its customers to believe about the project, they are now ready to define the major milestone encounters that must happen over this critical three-month period. How frequent do the major meetings have to be, and with whom in the client organization? What kind of substantive communication, in the form of follow-up communications, must happen in between these meetings, aiding the memory and understanding of the client?

Delta Partners determines that a weekly update meeting is necessary with all 15 people in the client organization who are involved.

These meetings will be a chance for an exchange of information, where Delta Partners can inform everyone about progress, but also hear the concerns of people and identify potential problem areas. Moreover, these sessions will help Delta Partners form relationships with the 10 managers who are not dedicated to the project team, and give Delta Partners a chance to read the impressions of those people. Delta Partners will suggest to the project team that these meetings occur Tuesday mornings, lasting for one hour.

Additionally, Delta Partners will suggest a Friday morning update meeting with the five dedicated members of the project team. This will be a chance to check in on progress since Tuesday's meeting, and to do some preparation in advance of next Tuesday's session. And, of course, this encounter in a smaller group is an opportunity to build relationships with these five key people.

Also, Delta Partners wants to schedule an interim milestone presentation to senior management two months from now and a final presentation just prior to the software cutover date.

This schedule of major milestones has been designed clearly to help realize the relationship's near-term "picture of success," by creating We encounters that encourage members of the client organization to believe certain things about the project and the relationship.

Fill in between the Milestones with Bridge Moments

> Neal Kusnetz is the president of Robert Graham, Inc., a high-end clothing label. I ask him, "Who is your best customer?" Neal tells me the name of a prominent, high-end retailer. "They are more than 20 percent of my business, and the relationship is very solid." "How often do you meet with them in person?" I inquire. "Four times a year. Every month we try to have a serious review meeting by telephone. But we have a lot of communication—a few short phone conversations every week, and probably at least one email every day. More when something big is happening, like the introduction of our new collection."

> If rich, milestone encounters are the building blocks of We relationships, bridge moments are the all-important mortar.

As noted earlier, we cannot always count solely on the major, milestone moments to create an adequate series of encounters that build a relationship. Neal Kusnetz recognizes that he must bridge the major encounters he has with his customer with less substantive encounters. These bridge encounters nurture his most important relationship in between the milestone moments.

In the case of Delta Partners' software upgrade, for which our story spans only 3 short months, Delta Partners must craft a series of smaller encounters to serve as a bridge between the milestones they have just defined. For example, short informal conversations every few days, either by telephone or in person at the client's office, can serve many important purposes. They can be an important chance to get client feedback, gauge what the client is thinking, and see how well he is remembering and understanding the content of previous encounters. They can also be an opportunity to fill in gaps of communication, giving an individual client personalized information that may not be communicated in a group meeting, and reminding him of key issues. It is most important, however, to recognize that these bridge encounters are not only functional, in terms of providing basic information and updates. They are important encounters in the building of relationships. If rich, milestone encounters are the building blocks of We relationships, bridge moments are the all-important mortar.

The same principle holds true over the longer term, especially when a relationship is not in such a critical, transitional period. There are many times in the course of a relationship where there are few needs` or opportunities for major, milestone encounters, and at these times it is important to craft bridge encounters that can keep the relationship's conversation continuous and its memories palpable. This is a critical issue for my consulting business when I am between projects with an ongoing client. We still have a relationship, but we may not have an opportunity to work together on a major project for a while. My challenge is to keep the relationship simmering, without interrupting my client with contacts that seem gratuitous, self-serving, and unimportant. To avoid falling into that trap, focus on the three elements of an encounter described earlier, which will help keep bridge encounters from degenerating into bothersome transactions:

- **No matter how minor the encounter, focus on making it a moment with presence.** A moment of full attention and engagement with a customer goes a long way.

- **Converse.** Don't waste this valuable time telling your story, or just letting your customer tell you what's up with him. Focus on a rich, interactive dialogue, even if it is only for a short time.

- **Make it unique.** Focus on things that are special to your customer and your relationship, and find ways to make these small moments special and different.

What makes bridge moments true encounters that build relationships is not how frequent they are or how long they last, but how much they follow the three elements of an encounter we discussed in Chapter 2.

The Beauty of the Ping

> Walking through Soho. I send a quick text message to my cousin. "Wish you were here. Just passed by your place. Saw a great concert at The Blue Note. Talk soon." We were both disappointed that he would be in L.A. during my trip to New York. Moments later, a message comes back. "Me too. In a production meeting drinking a Red Bull."

Ping! A short touch. A tiny connection. I don't pretend that it has moved the relationship forward in a significant way, but it *has* moved the relationship forward.

> **In an Us & Them relationship, a ping is spam.**

A ping is a special kind of bridge moment, designed to communicate a message as simple as "You matter to me." It is as simple, yet as valuable, as quickly stirring a pot on the stove. It takes only a moment, but it can add a spark to the momentum of the relationship.

Pings can be text messages, voicemail messages, emails, or, even better, short handwritten notes. You don't have to give them a lot of thought, but don't take them lightly. They matter.

After an encounter, a ping is a good, and appropriate, reinforcement. After a transaction, however, a ping is an annoyance. Similarly, in a We relationship, a ping is a reminder of what the relationship is all about. In an Us & Them relationship, a ping is spam.

THE CONTINUITY OF ENCOUNTERS BECOMES AN ONGOING CONVERSATION

Sam and I have been friends since age fourteen. We haven't lived in the same city for more than 20 years, but we keep in touch, speaking on the phone every few months and managing to get together in person once or twice a year. A number of years ago we fell into an interesting habit. When we start a phone conversation, even if it's been a while since we last talked, we start talking as if we were in the middle of a conversation. I answer the phone and hear him speaking in a normal voice: "You know, I agree with what you were saying about..." or, "We should go back to that Italian restaurant again some time." We do it to amuse ourselves, but, even more, it is a tacit that we've never really stopped our conversation.

Think of the best relationships in your life. Your best friends. Your closest family members. Your most productive and enjoyable business relationships. How many of these relationships are characterized by an ongoing conversation, a seamless dialogue that continues from encounter to encounter?

> Imagine a customer with whom your conversation never stops.

Conversation contributes to the building of a relationship as the dialogue in one encounter connects to the dialogue in other encounters, creating an ongoing conversation. With your best friends, don't you feel as if the conversation picks up right where it left off?

Let's imagine that you and a good friend each wrote down on a piece of paper the state of your ongoing conversation. You each list all the different topics that you talk about, and you each summarize the point your conversation is at on each of those topics. You'd be able to tell me your thoughts on each of those topics, and, also, what the other's thoughts are.

And, if it's a strong relationship, you'd probably both describe the ongoing conversation in a similar way.

What does it feel like to have an ongoing, continuous conversation with a customer that flows, seamlessly, through a series of encounters? Imagine a customer with whom your conversation never stops. Every time you reconnect with each other, you pick up right where you left off. There is an ongoing flow of interconnected, overlapping, and interweaving topics and ideas, all of which contribute to a rich story in which you both participate.

Continual vs. Continuous Conversations

The words continual and continuous have different meanings in English. "Continual" refers to a series of discrete, repeating events, while "continuous" refers to an uninterrupted, ongoing single event. (How to remember the difference: The "s" in continuous is like the sound of a hiss, which is a continuous sound.) Your series of encounters with a customer is, actually, a continual series of discrete events. What would it be like if you could create a continuous, unbroken conversation that weaves through that continual series of encounters? Imagine how it would feel to your customer if she felt as if the story of your relationship were always alive, always happening, always in process, even when you were not together.

The goal:
Continuous
conversation
within a
continual
series of
encounters.

The goal: Continuous conversation within a continual series of encounters.

A Shared Story Emerges from the Ongoing Conversation

When you first meet someone, you trade your individual stories as you get to know each other. After a series of encounters, as your relationship grows, you begin to supplement "my story" and "your story" with "our story." A shared story is a much more effective fuel for your relationship than your individual stories.

A shared story is a narrative, created together by you and your customer. It is not just about you, or just about your customer, but about both of you. It is a story in which you and your customers are active participants, active characters, and active authors.

Here is a fact we must all face: Our customers don't care much about our stories. They are much more interested in their own stories. Marketers and salespeople spend virtually all their resources on telling stories about themselves to customers and prospective customers. Is it any wonder that most companies' marketing and sales efforts are inefficient and unproductive?

How much more productive would your sales and marketing efforts be if, instead of telling stories about yourself to customers, you and your customer created, together, a shared story that involved both of you?

The idea of the shared story is, I believe, an idea that can be understood in terms of the recent history of marketing and sales. Throughout the last half of the twentieth century the practice of sales evolved from selling a product's features to selling the benefits of that product. This was an important step, because it recognized that the sale was not only about the product, but about what it did for the customer.

However, the focus on benefits was not enough. It became apparent to salespeople, and to people who thought about the process of sales, that not every customer cares about the same benefits. If you tell the scripted story of a product's benefits, it is a

> How much more productive would your sales and marketing efforts be if, instead of telling stories about yourself to customers, you and your customers created, together, a shared story that involved both of you?

crapshoot whether any particular customer would care about those benefits.

This brought on new ideas about how to ask questions to understand a customer's unique situation. Salespeople were looking for a way to "identify a customer's pain" so they could know what the customer needed most. We can think of this as an evolution from features and benefits to solutions, and it required salespeople to evolve from telling their stories to hearing the stories of their customers.

Philosophies of sales that teach salespeople to understand their customers, "identify their pain," and create customized solutions are a great leap forward. However, they still leave the salesperson with the challenge of connecting their company's solution to the customer's situation. No matter how good your solution is, and how well you explain that solution, it is possible that the customer won't see why it is best for him. Moreover, it is likely that an equally smart competitor can create the same solution for the same customer, after hearing the same story of pain from him.

This last phase had moved the practice of sales from telling "my story" to hearing "your story." The next leap forward is creating "our story." "Our story" is the shared story that is created by both of you, involves both of you, and gives you a shared context for understanding your relationship.

This idea of shared story matters to us in ways that go well beyond traditional sales and marketing. It is the joint narrative that defines the personality of a relationship.

In a shared story, each person sees his own reflection in the other. Weave your stories together in such a way that each time your customer sees you she sees a wonderful reflection of herself. This will then be a story she will much more easily remember. It is easier

> Go beyond "my story." Go beyond "your story." Create "OUR story."

for her to remember a story she is part of than a story only about someone else.

A shared story helps people see things in the same way. Go beyond "my story." Go beyond "your story." Find a way to create "our story."

Creating the Shared Story

When your relationship is young, it is natural for you and your customer each to bring your own, separate stories to your encounters. As your relationship begins to form, and as you develop an ongoing conversation, you begin to find places where your stories overlap, where your separate narratives can start to become intertwined into one shared story.

When you begin to understand each other's stories, you will see places where your stories can merge. As you get to know each other you can find the common details you share, the fine points of your character and personality that you have in common. These shared details are perfect points around which to build your shared story.

When I talk to a potential new client, my goal is not only for them to understand my story really well. I even view with equanimity a prospective client getting very excited during a conversation with me about the kinds of things I do. Why? Because I know this excitement will wane once I leave the prospective customer and she goes back to her life. In the midst of the hurricane of interruptions, obligations, commitments, and activities that she will face over the next 24 hours, it is likely that the detail, excitement, and nuance of my story will wear off, and she will, tomorrow, have only a general, watered-down recollection of my story.

If, however, our stories are woven together in a way that my customer can clearly envision herself working with me, she will see a shared story in which we participate together. Our encounter will be clear, compelling, and memorable.

Many of the techniques we have explored for creating encounters can be employed in this kind of situation, to help a new customer begin to envision a shared story with you. Bring the future forward by discussing scenarios in which you are working together. Help her participate in dialogical conversation with you, as you begin to weave together a shared narrative. And, of course, ensure that this conversation revolves around what makes you both unique, so you can both see how you fit together and complement each other.

The Never-ending Shared Story

Imagine a lifelong friendship. Over many years, the story shared between the participants in the relationship would grow, evolve, and be written. It would become richer, more interesting, and, most importantly, more shared. It would become an epic.

Great relationships are like epic narratives. Long-term, shared, epic narratives.

It may be easier to imagine a lifelong friendship than a lifelong customer relationship. But if we look at the shared story that develops over a long-term friendship, we can find inspiration about what can happen if a long-term customer relationship enjoys an epic, shared narrative. Aim high.

What an Ongoing Conversation Looks Like

An ongoing conversation has a few key features that are critical:

- **Picks up where it last left off.** When participants in a relationship reengage in a new encounter, they are more likely to enhance their relationship if their conversation continues from the point where it was at the end of their last meeting. As mentioned, memory helps bond one encounter to another. If that memory helps keep a conversation continuous, the relationship is likely to accelerate.

- **Shared story.** A shared story not only keeps interest high for the participants, it helps retain the flow of the conversation from one encounter to the next. This is because the shared story creates a shared frame of reference that allows the participants to reengage effectively when they come back together in an encounter.

⬤ **It rings true for the participants.** An ongoing conversation cannot retain its momentum unless it has strong relevance to those in the conversation. It must feel true, and it must feel important. In his book *Miscommunication*,[7] C. David Mortenson writes that a key to an ongoing conversation is to avoid a pileup of faulty assumptions. This is to keep integrity strong and truth high.

⬤ **It gets more interesting over time.** Have you ever noticed how much faster you read the second half of a good novel? Great stories become more compelling as they develop. Likewise, an ongoing conversation gets more interesting over time.

The 100th encounter with someone can be stale and boring, or can it be unique and more exciting than ever. In the best relationships, the story gains interest. Boredom is not a foregone conclusion. Each encounter, even after many encounters, has the possibility of being the most unique, the most special, moment the two of you have ever had. The story intensifies over time.

---

[7] C. David Mortensen, *Miscommunication* (Thousand Oaks, CA: Sage Publications, 1997), p. 15.

4

THE CONTINUITY DEVELOPS: REVEALING THE WAY WE COMPLEMENT EACH OTHER

YOUR RELATIONSHIP EVOLVES AS YOU HAVE
A CONTINUITY OF ENCOUNTERS.

AS YOUR RELATIONSHIP DEVELOPS,
YOU EACH BEGIN TO SEE HOW YOU FIT TOGETHER,
HOW YOU RELATE TO EACH OTHER.
HOW YOU COMPLEMENT EACH OTHER.

To Complement

As I get to know someone, or as my organization gets to know another organization, we begin to discover something very important: how we fit together. How we complement each other.

Of course, to complement each other does not mean you are identical. It is not necessarily to want the same things, to do the same things, or to enjoy the same things. It could be all of those, but it doesn't have to be.

To complement is to be mutually reinforcing. What is good for me is also good for you. What I do for me is good for you, and what I do for you is good for me. Our roles are complementary. We are complementary.

- The way we complement each other shows how we stand in relation to each other.

- The way we complement each other shows how we depend on each other.

- The way we complement each other shows why we are together.

From Competition to Complement

In our interviews, Dr. Jay Ferraro made the observation that couples who become divorced often tend to "keep score." For example, one might say "I took the kids last night, it's your turn tonight," or "Of course you should do the laundry, I make the money." They were in competition. On the other hand, the couples who are in happy marriages tend to focus more on how they complement each other, not on how they compete.

Of course, the same is true in business. If you and a customer compete for every dollar that is on the table, or for every precious day in a delivery schedule, the strength of your relationship is inherently limited. Once you begin to focus on how you complement each other, and not on how you compete, worlds open up for your relationship. The potential of your relationship becomes boundless.

> In a state of complement more is more.

In a state of competition, there is a fixed amount of benefit, over which the parties must fight. In a state of complement, more is more. When you win, I win. Once we see how we complement each other, how we fit together, our frame of reference is no longer what we can get from each other, but what we can do together.

Your Complement Is the Unique Personality of Your Relationship

Each pair of people or organizations who are in a relationship complement each other in a distinct way. No other two people or organizations would relate in the same way. Think of your best relationships, whether they are personal or business. You complement the other participants in one relationship in ways that are distinct from what happens in your other relationships. Each strong relationship brings out the best in you to fit together with what the relationship brings out in the other.

No two relationships ever have been, or ever will be, identical. Each pair of people or organizations that enter into a relationship complement each other in a way that is unique to them. How they fit together is the true determinant of what their relationship is.

The Continuity of Encounters Reveals Our Complement

In Chapter 3, we discussed how a relationship forms from a continuity of encounters. The personality of a relationship, as defined by the unique nature of the way the participants complement each other, comes to life as this continuity develops.

Consider how a strong personal friendship evolves. During the early encounters that form a relationship, two people do not know each other well, but they begin to sense that there is potential in the relationship. They see early signs that they "fit" together well. Their complement begins to reveal itself in terms that, later, seem simple. At the time, however, this simple complement is interesting enough to encourage them to continue the relationship. As time progresses, and they have more and more encounters, both begin to see much richer ways that they complement each other. Now, looking back, they can see how the ongoing continuity of encounters they have created together reveals the rich, multi-faceted ways in which they complement each other.

The same thing happens with long-lasting business relationships. Early on, the participants in the relationship see simple ways that they complement each other. A customer has a need, the seller has a product. But, years later, they can complement each other in ways that go well beyond the product and the need for that product. That mutual understanding of their complement doesn't come out of nowhere; it is revealed through the ongoing series of encounters they have together.

COMPLEMENTARY UNDERSTANDING, GOALS, ACTIONS, OUTCOMES

WE UNDERSTAND HOW WE COMPLEMENT.
WE WANT THINGS THAT ARE IN COMPLEMENT.
WE DO THINGS THAT ARE IN COMPLEMENT.
WE ENJOY OUTCOMES THAT ARE IN COMPLEMENT.

As we come to know each other and our relationship, we will develop a mutual understanding of each other's identity, and what that means to the way we can relate to each other.

Once we develop this complementary understanding, we will come to understand our complementary goals. We will each come to believe that what is good for one is good for the other.

These goals lead to complementary action. In pursuit of our complementary goals, we act in ways that are mutually reinforcing.

These complementary actions lead to complementary outcomes. We both benefit from each other's success. When our outcomes are in complement, we see clearly how our relationship is of value, and that its value derives from We, two unique participants, complementing each other. We become "We."

COMPLEMENTARY   COMPLEMENTARY   COMPLEMENTARY   COMPLEMENTARY

understanding   goals   actions   outcomes

WHO   ⇨   WHAT   ⇨   WHAT   ⇨   WHAT
we are   we want   we do   we enjoy

COMPLEMENTARY UNDERSTANDING: WE KNOW EACH OTHER IN RELATION TO OURSELVES

In our earlier discussion of the third element of an encounter, uniqueness, we recognized that every person and every organization in the world is unique. In every encounter, it is necessary to meet the other person as a unique individual.

Although it is possible to encounter someone as a unique person the first time you meet him, the uniqueness you recognize in an early encounter only scratches the surface of that person's individual, human identity. As your relationship develops through a series of encounters, it is possible to learn new things about that person that were impenetrable to you in your earliest meetings. You get to know him.

Similarly, this other person gets to know you. As you learn about each other, you begin to recognize characteristics you share and characteristics you do not share. Both are critical to the unique way you complement each other.

Connect "Uniquenesses," One by One

It is easy to be awestruck by the uniqueness of each person on earth. Look at any person and know that there has been, and never will be, another person just like that. Every person who has lived or will live is a rich, complex, interesting array of features, characteristics, interests, strengths, tempos, temperaments, and delights that will appear on earth only once. Yet, as we discussed, it is only the last one-half of one percent that makes us unique. The other 99.5 percent of our genetic code is shared with the rest of humanity.

> **What makes them special are the features of their character and company personality.**

As your relationship develops with someone, you each will begin to recognize more components of that half of one percent, the fine details and spices that make each of you a special person. The more you know each other, the more you can discern each other's unique details.

The same holds true with organizations. If, on one day, you were to meet two companies who were in the same industry, they may seem quite similar to you. However, as you become better acquainted with each of them, you begin to see that each is defined by nuances and detail that go well beyond the products they make and sell. What makes them special are the features of their character and company personality, which are driven by many things, the most powerful of which are the people in the organization. This recognition of their "uniquenesses" may have been invisible to you on the day you met them, but after many encounters can be clearly seen.

The uniqueness that connects you and your customer in a relationship has two facets:

1) **Special characteristics you both share**...
   the fine details you have in common

2) **Special characteristics you do not share**...
   the fine details you do not have in common, but that help you complement each other

Look for the details you share

My friend is called into the IRS for a tax audit. On the day of her appointment, she is ushered into the office of a woman who seems foreboding, disinterested, and bureaucratic. On first blush, the situation doesn't seem promising.

They start talking. The conversation is officious, stiff, and cold. Suddenly, my friend notices knitting needles sticking out of the woman's purse. "You like knitting?" Immediately, they launch into a ten-minute conversation about knitting, giving each other advice and sharing their common passion.

When they return to the subject of taxes, things are different. Now, they talk as real people. They know each other. Knitting is only one item in the rich panorama of each of their lives. But it is something they share.

A person with whom you develop a relationship may be, on the surface (or on their driver's license), very different from you. Age, gender, background, political leanings—you name it, you don't have many of those in common.

But beyond basic demographics, there may be many things you do have in common, many distinct features that you share. In many cases, they will be business-related, and these, obviously, can help you create a bridge to a relationship. If your company has a special expertise in a certain area, and you discover that your customer requires this special expertise, this is an obvious opportunity to add a unique dimension to your relationship. Or maybe you own a restaurant, and you learn about a particular dislike one of your best customers has for cardamom; your chef's fluency with spices will help you address this detail of your customer's personality.

However, don't sell short the non-business things you may have in common. As with my friend and the IRS agent, the unique features from your personal lives can also help you forge an important connection. Maybe you speak a common foreign language. Maybe you share a favorite vacation spot. Or own the same kind of dog. These may seem unrelated to the business at hand, but they can be important links that help connect your relationship.

Sara Silver, owner of the software firm Silverware, is visiting a new client's office. This is their third meeting since Silverware began a project to revamp the client's accounting

> Part of your job is to understand your client (and yourself) well enough to spot shared, unique features.

systems. Sara and her client, Lisa Stern, are developing a nice warm relationship, but, so far, it's all business.

At a break, Lisa asks Sara to walk with her to her office to get something so they can continue their conversation. Sara's first reaction as she walks into Lisa's office is that it could be her own. Bruce Springsteen posters, framed Springsteen concert ticket stubs, and other Bruce paraphernalia fill the office. She stops dead in her tracks. "Oh, my God. I can't believe it." Sara recognizes immediately that she and Lisa are both Springsteen fanatics. Within moments they are discussing tour dates—they have been to more than 50 concerts between the two of them, and have probably been to 15 of the same concerts, dancing to the music in different parts of the auditorium. They realize that they both have tickets to a concert in L.A. next week, and they're pretty sure that they are on the same Southwest flight from Phoenix to LAX on Wednesday. They are discussing their favorite songs and beginning to share some of the obscure facts about the music that they know.

Over the next three years, Sara and Lisa travel cross-country to Springsteen concerts together 12 times. Every time Springsteen comes to Phoenix they go together with Sara's sons, who now know Lisa personally. When a new record comes out, they make sure that their first listening experience is together.

Part of your job is to understand your client (and yourself) well enough that you can spot these shared, unique features, and, in a genuine way, integrate them into your relationship. Sara got lucky—Lisa's office was covered with Springsteen paraphernalia. It would have been hard *not* to notice what they shared. Be alert to notice those similarities that are not so obvious—whether it be a business uniqueness or a personal one. However, similarities are not the only characteristics of value in developing your relationships.

Look for Details You Do Not Share

L.A. studio musician Miriam Clarke is working in a recording studio, adding flute parts to a piece a friend has composed. As she listens to a playback of what she has recorded, she says to the recording engineer, Ron Pendragon, "My flute sounds a little dry, like I'm playing in a small room. Can we add a little more reverb to my flute so it sounds like it's in a real concert setting?" He says, "Sure. We can use the reverb sound of the Mozart Hall in Salzburg or the Sydney Opera House. They're both options on the digital reverb on my computer, and I think either could work. Let's try them." Miriam was thinking at the general level of "reverb," and Ron was thinking at a much different level of detail. He was able to focus on which reverb. At the same time, however, Miriam was thinking of the details and nuances of the flute melody with great care and detail, so Ron didn't have to worry about the flute part. By trusting each other's expertise, each was able to focus on what they were responsible for.

One of the things that most distinguishes humans from the rest of the animal kingdom is the way members of our species specialize. All squirrels have basically the same job. The ability that humans have to divide up the work opens worlds of possibilities.

One of the best ways to collaborate with someone is for each of you to focus on different pieces of the project at hand. This division of labor is exactly what should happen as you forge a relationship with a customer. Your relationship does not have to be inherently one-sided, as is traditionally assumed in buyer/seller relationships. ("We do it all for you!") You both bring important things to the party, and one of the best ways to move from doing things *for* your customers to doing things *with* your customers is to look for the ways you complement each other.

> As opposed to selling each other, look for how you can work together.

It's as simple as this: As opposed to selling each other, look for how you can work together.

The natural human tendency is for us to value things in others that match our own strengths. As an example, think about what happens when two job candidates are paraded through a series of interviews in an office, one of them being a left-brained hyper-organized type, and the other being a right-brained scattered-creative person. The organized, left-brained interviewer will like the candidate who is most like him, and the right-brained creatives will like the other candidate.

We are much better off, however, if we find ways to work with people who are different than we are. Many of my clients are senior marketing executives, who have responsibility for large departments and large budgets, and they spend a lot of their time navigating the labyrinth of corporate politics. I've done all that, and, thank you, I'm more than happy that I don't do it anymore. I can add the most value by complementing the work of these people. We have different strengths, and the differences add strength to our relationship.

Recognizing What You Know About Your Customer

Alberto Was is a contract manufacturer of men's clothing. His factory in Uruguay produces clothing for several well-known Latin American labels whose products are sold from Mexico to Chile.

Alberto describes one of his best We relationships. "I had been doing business with Alejandro Szuldman and his company, J. Nicols, for seven years. Their focus had been on selling pants, and they had done quite well. But as I got to know their business, I realized that they had a great opportunity to move into men's suits. They had the right styles and the right retail customers, and I knew they could make a lot more money in suits than they did in pants. The profit margins are a lot better. At first, my client resisted me. He didn't see the possibility. But I kept on him. I knew enough about his business to know that he could be successful. Finally, he agreed to a small test. We created some prototype garments, and I accompanied him on sales calls to key customers. Now, as they say, the rest is history. Most of his profit comes from suits, and he does significantly more business with me."

Alberto recognized special things about his customer, and he showed the customer that he recognized these things. His understanding of his customer fueled the growth of the relationship. Alberto didn't just try to sell his customer on moving into men's suits. His knowledge of his customer helped him recognize a business opportunity for his customer.

How well do you really know your customers?

> Understanding drives We, and We leads to further understanding.

If your customers are businesses...Do you know what their business strategy is? Do you know whether they have a solid business strategy or not? Do you know what makes their customers love them...or not love them? Do you understand the personality of their company? Do you understand the personalities of the people you deal with within their company?

If your customers are consumers...Do you know who they are— really know who they are? How well do you know them? Do you know what makes them tick, what interests them?

My observation is this: Companies in We relationships tend to understand each other very well. Cause and effect are bi-directional and mutually reinforcing; understanding drives We, and We leads to further understanding.

NOTICE>> Look at companies you do business with, both in your personal and business lives. How good are they at understanding their customers? How well do they know their customers? How well do they know you?

HOW DO YOU COMPARE>> How well do you and your organization understand your customers? (*Really* understand your customers?)

Helping Your Customer Recognize Things About You

Over the years I have had interactions with thousands of executives in the course of my workshops, seminars, and consulting. One of the most common frustrations I have heard is this: "Our customers don't even know what we sell. They only know about the things they buy from us, and don't consider us for the other things we could do." Executives with this complaint come from all sorts of companies: manufacturers, law firms, distributors—you name it.

It is no surprise to me when I hear executives complain that their customers don't understand them when I consider the means by which most companies communicate with their customers.

Companies pour out messages to the marketplace, describing their latest products, touting their latest promotions, telling their customers things of dubious interest to them, such as "Since 1986." They look at marketing and branding as exercises to "get the word out" and create awareness.

Despite the large fortunes companies spend on marketing, most companies fail to communicate the kinds of things that can create strong customer relationships. As described in my book *Brand Harmony*, the traditional model of marketing over the last fifty-plus years has been one of brute force; i.e., that the way to persuade customers to do business with you is to bombard them as many times as possible with messages that are as powerful as possible.

Brute force, as a marketing and branding method, is used to "cut through the clutter" and get a customer's attention. It is not designed to tell a rich story about you and your company. Brute force marketing tools, such as advertising, direct mail, sales promotions, etc., are one-way communications, and all they talk about is the seller. As such, they are only of limited interest to the buyer, and the buyer will only retain general information after coming in contact with these communications. Marketing and sales efforts that just pitch products are not conversations that help a customer understand the soul of the company.

> **"What is it we want people to think/know about us?"** This question is very different from **"What do we want to say about ourselves?"**

Instead of thinking about what you want to say to customers, focus first on what you want them to know about you. I am convinced that most companies fail to ask this very simple question: "What is it we want people to think/know about us?" This question is very different from "What do we want to say about ourselves?"

When you throw mounds of information at your customer, you depend on the customer to add it all together and form a composite idea of who you are. This leaves a lot to chance. The personality of your company is too important, too interesting, and too rich to be left to that chance.

Be careful and deliberate as you craft your personality. Think prudently about who you want to be and how you want to be considered. Reveal what you want to reveal to your customers, not what gets revealed by default. Make it possible to be clearly and easily known.

Your Complementary Understanding Is Revealed

The details you share in common, and those you don't share, the things you recognize about your customer and those your customer recognizes about you—all of these add up to your complementary understanding of each other and of your relationship.

This mutual self-recognition is a critical step in the development of your We relationship. It is where you begin to understand the unique way you fit together, the unique way you relate to each other.

Let the ongoing series of encounters reveal this complementary understanding. It will be a strong voice in the shared story that is emerging, and both of you notice it if you are alert to its message. Simply put, if you are engaged in rich We encounters you will not have to force this complementary understanding to emerge; it will reveal itself naturally.

This complementary understanding makes possible the next step in the development of your We relationship: complementary goals.

COMPLEMENTARY GOALS: WE BELIEVE THAT WHAT IS GOOD FOR ONE IS GOOD FOR THE OTHER

WE MAY NOT WANT THE SAME THINGS, BUT WE WANT EACH OTHER TO DO WELL. WHY IS THIS? WHAT MAKES IT HAPPEN?

Interest in Each Other's Success

Do your customers want you to succeed?
Do they care?
What would make them care?

Steve Pinetti, senior vice-president of sales and marketing for Kimpton Hotels & Restaurants, calls a top customer, who not only stays at Kimpton Hotels frequently, but also refers a lot of business to Kimpton. "I really appreciate that you've brought us so many customers. I want to take you to dinner to thank you," Steve says. "I'd love to go to dinner," responds the customer, "just name the time. But you don't have to take me. We're going dutch." "Please," Steve continues, "you've done so much for us." "I refer business to you," the customer continued, "because I really want you guys to have the business. I really want you to do well. It makes me feel good to help you."

How many of your customers care if you succeed?
How many of your customers would be concerned—*really* concerned—if they thought your business was in trouble?
How many would be happy—*really* happy—if they found out you had great success?
A sure sign that a relationship is moving from the world of Us & Them to the realm of We is that each party begins to care deeply, and genuinely, for the other's success and well-being.

Author and psychologist Hendrie Weisinger tells me about his experience working with "Million Dollar Roundtable" events, in which top insurance sellers gather together to learn and share ideas. "The top salespeople in insurance are always the people who really believe that what they are doing is helping people have a better life, by protecting their futures or preventing them from facing some sort of catastrophe. The people who just look at selling insurance as a way to make money are never as successful."

Consider your best friendships. Aren't you really happy when you hear about something good that happened to a friend? Aren't you really sad when you hear that something bad happened to a friend?

In a We business relationship the same is true. Partners in a We relationship, both buyer and seller, care deeply about what happens to the other. There are two reasons for this.

The first is purely altruistic. We want people whom we like to do well.

The second is very practical (but still 100 percent genuine). We believe that the success of people with whom we are in We relationships is also to our benefit.

I mean what I say: This feeling is 100 percent genuine. There is nothing wrong with a customer's wanting me to succeed because, in addition to her pure interest in my success, she believes that my success is good for her. And there is nothing wrong with my wanting my customers to succeed because, in addition to my pure interest in seeing them succeed, it will also benefit me.

> **We believe that the success of people with whom we are in We relationships is also to our benefit.**

Why is this self-interest still genuine? Recognizing that I benefit through your success is acknowledgment that we have a relationship. After all, if I didn't benefit at all from your success, we must not be connected. But if I were in a We relationship with you, I would believe that our fates are tied together. I would believe that what is good for one of us is good for both of us. Our goals are complementary because our successes are mutually rein-forcing. We are interdependent with each other and bonded to each other. It is a sign that our relationship has meaning. It has real sub-stance and staying power.

Us & Them relationships are based on a zero-sum idea, that your win is my loss. Not so with We relationships, where complementary goals prove the principle of the abundance mentality, i.e., that there is enough for both of us.

There is a moment in time where you recognize your interde-pendency and complementary attributes. This is a wonderful moment, because it signifies an important stage in the development of your We relationship. Savor it. Your relationship has become something new and different.

Learn Your Customer's Goals

Do you know your customers' goals? What are they really trying to accomplish by doing business with you?

Can you articulate, with clarity and confidence, why your cus-tomer does business with you?

I don't just mean the first-level reasons you might cite, such as "they need my product," or "we deliver on time." Dig deeper. Do you know—really know—what they are trying to accomplish in their rela-tionship with you? How do you fit into the really important issues they face in their business and life? What do they get out of the rela-tionship?

What Every Fortune 500 Company Can Learn from My Dry Cleaners

I have used the same dry cleaners for years. Jim Dandy Cleaners shows up, without fail, every Tuesday and Friday morning to drop off clean clothes and pick up a new load that needs cleaning. One Thursday night last summer I re-turned from a three-week trip out of the country, and I had to leave again Sunday night for the West Coast. On Friday morning, I stuck the dirty clothes in the blue Jim Dandy bag, and put the bag on the front porch. Later in the day I realized I'd want some of that clothing for my trip, but they weren't scheduled to be returned until Tuesday. I called Jim Dandy, and the owner's daughter answered the phone. I told her I needed some of the pieces of clothing they had for an upcoming business trip, and asked if it was possible for me to get them by Saturday afternoon. "I'll run in the back right now and see if I can find your clothes. They're in the group to be cleaned on Monday, but I'll bet I can find them. Let me know if you can't get here by five tomorrow when we close, because I can leave them at the store next door for you." Relief. I'll have my clothes. The next morning at about 8:30 I got a call from Jim Dandy. "We're delivering your clothes in about an hour." Wow. Was this good customer service? Of course. But calling it "good customer service" sells it short. It was way beyond customer service. I truly believe that *the people at Jim Dandy sincerely wanted me to have my clothes for my business trip.*

Jim Dandy Cleaners recognized my goals; it was so obvious to me that the owner's daughter's real interest was that I have my clothes. She was thinking of my goal, not hers. Genuineness like this cannot be faked. There are certain things you just know, and this was one of them.

Help Your Customers Discover Their Goals

One of my favorite things about management consulting is helping my clients find ways to succeed that they hadn't recognized previously. People often call me with a specific need they want to address. It may be a problem of brand awareness, or it may be a marketing department that isn't functioning well, or they may state a need for better sales materials. Frequently, once I start digging into the client's situation, I see that their description of their problem doesn't fully describe the issues that concern them. They are unable to articulate fully what the problem is. The brand awareness problem may actually be a reaction to the popularity of a more prominent

> **When you help your customer define important goals that were not evident before, you have made yourself a significantly more valuable partner in the relationship.**

competitor, which can be addressed in a more effective way than a major investment in building brand awareness. Or, the client with a poorly per-forming marketing department may think that this problem can be solved with reorganization and prioritization, when in reality what he really needs is a better process for making marketing decisions. The client who wants better sales materials may really just be reacting to the yelps and cries of a sales force that can't articulate the company's brand story through conversation. Helping a customer define goals he hasn't yet recognized is very valuable to that customer.

This can happen in many businesses. When a waiter helps you create a dinner experience you hadn't conceived of, or when an architect creates a plan that was beyond your dreams—all of these show the power of identifying a customer's goals for her.

When her goal is identified, the customer will not only credit you, she will connect her success to you. Her success is your success, and it is only a small step from there for her to think that your success is her success. When you create goals with your customer, they are much more likely to be complementary.

Consultant Alan Weiss describes the difference between a structured problem and an unstructured problem. With a structured problem, a customer knows exactly what he needs. The only value he wants from you is to fulfill those stated needs. With an unstruc-tured problem, however, a customer doesn't know what he needs, and you add a great deal of value by helping him discover those needs. When you help your customer define important goals that were not evident before, as in the examples above, you have made yourself a significantly more valuable partner in the relationship.

Earlier I described a situation that happened to Joe Honor, vice president of VMC Behavioral Health Care Services. A client inter-rupted a sales presentation with a problem unrelated to content of the presentation. In that story, Joe described how he was willing to stop the presentation and engage with the client in a discussion of his tangential issue, in order to demonstrate how important it is to say "Yes" to the direction a customer wants to take in a conversation. What Joe learned in this conversation was that the client had only a basic idea of what his problem was, and a limited recognition of the solutions available. "Through our conversation, we brainstormed and were able to find a way to create an innovative, fresh solution that addressed his problem in a way that he didn't know was possible. He and his team had no idea that a solution like this was available and really didn't understand the extent of the benefit to them if they fixed this problem." Joe's conversation, which represented a departure from the planned meeting agenda, helped reframe the problem for the customer and redefine the customer's goals related to this issue. The client better understood his own goals, and credited Joe with it. "The client later told me that he had presented this problem to a number of our competitors, but each of them had answered with stock, canned answers that were based more on that company's products than what the customer needed. We worked really hard to understand what the client really wanted, and he noticed that. The sale we made that day was four times what we had expected to sell, and three years later we have an incredible strong relationship with this client."

Do Your Customers Know Your Goals?

Do your customers understand your goals? Do they know what you would like to accomplish in your business, and, particularly, from your relationship with them?

Your first reaction may be this: "Why would my customers care about my goals?"

To which I reply: They will never care about your goals if they do not know what those goals are. As your relationship develops, it will become more and more appropriate to discuss your goals with your customer. She will be receptive to this conversation, because she will have more interest in you. Don't be afraid to share your goals with your customer; they are important to you, and, hence, they are becoming more important to her.

Of course, you cannot discuss complementary goals too early in your relationship. That would be forced. As your relationship develops, your respective goals will naturally begin to intertwine. At that point, you can help your customer acknowledge this fact through your ongoing conversation. Your goals are important, too. Do not be reticent in sharing them.

Bring the Goals of Both into the Shared Story

Complementary goals are an overlapping double beacon in the distance, guiding you both to the same destination. Both sets of goals are visible to each of you. They become a constant in your relationship. They become a resonant theme in your shared story.

As you begin to understand and acknowledge each other's goals, you can help your customer see them as complementary by weaving them into the shared story that drives your ongoing conversation. Look for places where your goals complement each other's and, when appropriate, discuss your goals at the same time you are discussing your customer's goals. You want your customer to think of your goals and hers in the same thought.

> Jim, a real estate lawyer, describes a relationship with a client: "I've focused most of my practice on residential multi-family and commercial retail deals. I've wanted to break into the lodging sector for a while, helping people buy and sell hotels, but I hadn't found the right opportunity. At one point, a client of mine, Bill, mentioned he was looking to purchase some hotels. In the course of the conversation I realized that he hadn't ever connected me with this work, because he hadn't ever thought about me doing that kind of work. Over the course of our next conversations, I shared with him my interest in the hotel business. As we discussed it, it became clear to both of us that our goals in the hotel business reinforced each other. He wanted to buy hotels; I

wanted to do the legal work. Not the same goals, but compatible goals."

By developing a shared story that included their complementary goals, Jim and his client found a path to a stronger We relationship.

Your Complementary Goals Are Revealed

As with your complementary understanding, your complementary goals will emerge naturally as your relationship develops. They will start simply, and become more pronounced and more important over time.

Be alert to your complementary goals as you have encounters with your customer. They are twin beacons leading you both to the same future.

But complementary goals are not an end result. They guide complementary action.

COMPLEMENTARY ACTIONS: WE DO THINGS THAT ARE MUTUALLY REINFORCING

When people see that their goals are complementary, they will begin to do things that benefit each other.

As we discussed earlier, one of the unique features of the human species is that we specialize and divide up the work. Once two parties in a relationship begin to understand their complementary goals, whether they are individuals or organizations, they will begin to act in complementary ways to reach those goals.

Complementary Actions and the We Encounter

People often act in complementary ways in Us & Them relationships. A wealthy estate owner pays his gardener a fair wage, and the gardener tends to the plants. Their actions complement each other, but their relationship remains distant.

Complementary actions in a We relationship are not so separate. They are interlaced in a fine weave, even within individual encounters. The We encounter is one in which we do things *with* each other,

> Your individual actions are intertwined and inter- dependent.

not only *for* each other. To do something *with* someone does not mean that you do identical things. It means that your individual actions are intertwined and interdependent.

A good example of this is when I collaborate with a client on a presentation for his or her management team. We work with each other, dividing up the work into fine, interlaced, interdependent pieces. By the time the presentation is done, it is impossible to distinguish our individual contributions. They have become "our" contributions. The presentation is "our" presentation.

So, even though we divide up the work in a We relationship, our actions are still closely related and collaborative. Sure, there is much work in a We relationship that happens when the participants are separated by both time and place, but it is always clear that our actions are collaborative. We don't just do things *for* each other, we do things *with* each other.

We Work Towards Your Goals, and We Work Towards Mine

"Teamwork" is such an overused term that we often forget its real meaning. It is often understood to mean working together without friction, but it is more than that. It is about how we allocate the work based on our respective strengths and abilities.

The essence of complementary action in a We relationship is that many of my actions are directed towards your goals, and many of yours are directed towards mine. And, many of our joint, collaborative actions are directed at only one of our goals.

Interdependency Strengthens Our Bond

As we collaborate to help each other, we see clear evidence of why we are in our relationship. We come to understand how our complementary actions reinforce each other. Good relationships have a healthy interdependency. We lean on each other, not as crutches, but for a strength and stability that allows each of us to accomplish more than we could on our own.

Opportunities for Complementary Action: Outsourcing and Joint Teams

> When your customer allows you to become part of his organization and collaborate as a member of his team, you will have created opportunities for We encounters and relationship-building opportunities your competitors could only dream of.

The anxious debate on outsourcing in recent years misses the most interesting parts of this issue. For every task that is outsourced to a foreign country, as with call centers and software coding, hundreds of tasks are outsourced to offices down the street. Why have your own travel department when a local travel agency can do it for you? Why hire information technology specialists when there are scores of companies within miles of your location who would like to take this responsibility off your hands?

When your customer allows you to become part of his organization and collaborate as a member of his team, you will have created opportunities for We encounters and relationship-building opportunities with this customer that your competitors could only dream of.

The challenge, however, is earning the right to be thought of as a part of your customer's organization. As numerous as the sands on the seashore are the professional service firms who say, "We want to be our customer's outsourced accounting/marketing/insurance/ IT/HR/maintenance department." Just saying this doesn't do anything. What makes it happen?

A collaborative relationship like this, where a customer relies on you for functions that he could have on his own payroll, is a We relationship. Like all We relationships, it cannot be promised in brochures or described on a website. It is built through a series of relationship-building encounters, over time. Rob Shell, president of Prism Innovations, a company that provides Cisco Systems' SMARTnet contract management, told me about the relationship he has with his outsourced marketing services provider, Brian Kovach of Symbiotic Marketing. "Brian has been working with me the entire time I've been in business, which is more than seven years. I don't think we ever planned it this way, but as we have worked together, he has become an integral part of the team. Our relationship has grown through the work we've done together. During that time we have had hundreds of conversations about the business, and how to grow the business. I've come to rely on him." In other words, Brian created his We relationship with Rob not through promises, but through encounters.

Rob describes how their relationship has evolved into complementary actions. "Brian and I have different strengths. Over time, we figured out what we each do best, and that's how we work together. I come up with lots of ideas, and I bring them to Brian. He helps me translate my ideas into action, which is something I couldn't do without his help." Rob's and Brian's actions are complementary and mutually reinforcing.

David Baker, president of Baker Robbins, an international knowledge management consulting firm serving the legal industry, found a good steppingstone to this kind of interdependent relationship: A joint inter-company team focused on a particular project. "The reality is that many of our large projects can't succeed without deep involvement from both people on my team and people on the client's team. The traditional way to deal with this is for the consulting company to manage things, and ask the client for task-specific information and help. We've found that it is much more productive to create joint teams, consisting of people from both companies. This creates a better situation. After a while, a casual observer looking in from the outside would have a hard time telling who was from which company."

> "A casual observer looking in from the outside would have a hard time telling who was from which company."

This kind of collaboration shows the customer what it's like to work *with* you, not just have you work *for* them. The encounters that occur in a situation like this make deeper collaboration not only possible, but expected.

Charles Dann, a partner in the prominent Chicago-area firm Dann Insurance, describes how he and his team build relationships in this way. "Most of our clients cannot afford their own risk managers. Through our ongoing relationship, we convey to the client that we're his insurance department. Then, we're not thought of as just some remote organization. We're part of his organization."

Earlier, we described complementary goals as bright beacons that help us see the value of our relationship in the distance. Complementary actions bring the sight of this value much closer, and much more in focus. When I see you acting on my behalf, and when you see me acting on your behalf, our bond of We is strengthened. We both begin to see that it is "We" who are doing things, not just "You and I." And, importantly, it is "We" who benefit.

COMPLEMENTARY OUTCOMES: WE BOTH BENEFIT FROM EACH OTHER'S SUCCESS

> **Complementary actions create complementary results.**

Goals do not create results, although they provide invaluable direction. Action creates results. Complementary actions create complementary results.

Tangible Results Make a Relationship Tangible

Imagine working closely with an architect building a new home, forging a strong We relationship in the process. Wouldn't that relationship hit a new high the first night you spend in the house, enjoying the fruits of your collaborative labors?

We spoke earlier about how complementary goals are beacons in the distance to which we both aim our travels, and that complementary actions give us a much closer, clearer sight of the value of our relationship. Results show the value of our relationship in an even clearer way. By giving us a tangible benefit, results make the relationship itself more tangible.

What It Means for Outcomes to Be Complementary

> My client called to tell me his company just had its best month of the year. I was happy for him. But I was also happy for me.

It is possible to derive benefits from an Us & Them relationship. For example, I have an Us & Them relationship with Costco, and enjoy benefits from them in the form of discounts on my shopping. What makes a We relationship different, however, is that in a We relationship our outcomes are interdependent on the success of the other. In an Us & Them relationship, it is possible for one party to succeed independent of the other.

Costco benefits from my success with one of their products only in the sense that I may buy more from them, or recommend them to my friends. However, Costco does not benefit from my general success. In fact, if I have significant success, Costco may suffer if I don't feel the need to drive an extra 15 minutes to save a few bucks.

This is a fundamental and critical difference between a We relationship and an Us & Them relationship. In an Us & Them relationship we may benefit from what others do, but in a We relationship we also benefit when the other enjoys benefits. The actual fact of one's success is good for the other, in a very direct way.

As we discussed earlier, in a We relationship I want my customer to succeed for altruistic reasons, but I also want my customer to succeed because it is good for me. There is nothing disingenuous about this second reason. In fact it is very powerful; recognizing that I benefit from your success acknowledges the bond of our relationship. We are interdependent not only in our goals and actions, but in the complementary results we enjoy.

We Can Trace Our Success to the Other's Actions

> In a We relationship, we can trace our success directly to the actions of specific individual customers.

When a business derives its results from many Us & Them relationships, it tends to measure its success on the aggregate actions of groups of customers. "Seventeen percent of our customers spent over $100 per transaction," or "We served 175 people for dinner last night, 37 of whom ordered the chef's special entrée."

With We relationships, however, we can trace our success directly to the actions of specific, individual customers. And, importantly, they can trace their success directly to actions we undertook within our relationships with them. We credit each other for our success, and we both recognize how we have helped the other. We have a clear, mutual understanding of the value that our We relationship provides to both of us.

Belief in Abundance: Plenty of Outcomes for All

> Benefits for one create new possibilities and opportunities for the other.

As we have noted previously, Us & Them relationships are based largely on the idea of finite benefits, while We relationships are based on the idea of abundance. In a We relationship, benefits are not scarce and do not have to be divided up among us. In fact, the direct opposite is true; benefits for one create new possibilities and opportunities for the other.

5

WE AMONG MANY: RELATIONSHIPS BETWEEN ORGANIZATIONS

ORGANIZATIONAL RELATIONSHIPS
ARE BUILT FROM
INDIVIDUAL RELATIONSHIPS

Consider the following two scenarios:

SCENARIO 1: A salesperson develops a strong We relationship with a client, built on a series of encounters. However, every time this client interacts with another person in the salesperson's company, it is transactional. After a period of time, the salesperson leaves the company. Does the client continue to do business with this company?

SCENARIO 2: A salesperson develops a strong We relationship with a client, built on a series of encounters. Over time, this client has encounters with many other people in the salesperson's company, which support and complement the encounters the client has with the salesperson. After a period of time, the salesperson leaves the company. Does the client continue to do business with this company?

If a customer has We encounters with multiple people in an organization, and develops We relationships with a number of those people, he will start to believe he has a We relationship with the organization, in addition to the individual people who represent the organization.

Time and again in our work at Yastrow Marketing, our research shows that strong relationships a customer has with an organization are built on relationships with individual people within that organization. The happiest customers will always mention the greatest number of employees by name, and will describe rich encounters with those employees.

Chapter 6 of my book *Brand Harmony* is called "Be the Brand." This chapter describes the powerful effect that individual employees in a company can have on a customer's brand impression, and describes a method for helping employees "be the brand" every day on the job. Even the most highly automated companies live and die on the actions of their people, including those whose products are made in dark, virtually unmanned, robotic factories. Products and robots are predictable and consistent. People are not. In order to

> A relationship between two organizations has its roots in strong We relationships between individuals.

create We relationships between your organization and its customers, it is important that the people who work in the company understand what kind of We relationships you are trying to create with customers.

The concept of Brand Harmony explains why this is so. A customer's evaluation of a company, its products, or its services is based on the way all interactions with that company blend, in harmony or dissonance, to communicate a story for that customer. Since all interactions with the company fuel this evaluation, every employee, even those without customer contact, have an impact on the customer experience, and, subsequently, on the customer's brand impression. Multiple We relationships with a company, along with other supplemental experiences, will blend in Brand Harmony to create an overall, rich, integrated feeling of We.

"Be the Brand" happens when employees eagerly and actively participate in the communication of a brand story with customers. I have spent a great deal of time over the years working with companies to make this happen, and my observation and belief is that most employees want to "Be the Brand." If they aren't acting in concert with the company's brand strategy, it can usually be traced to a few key reasons, most notably that no one has ever talked to them about being the brand, and that there are obstacles *preventing* them from being the brand.

Encouraging employees to create We encounters and encouraging them to form We relationships are very similar. Most of them will want to do it, but it is necessary to address the following key principles:

1) Ensure that employees understand how to create We relationships

2) Ensure that employees can create We relationships

> "Be the Brand" happens when employees eagerly and actively participate in the communication of a brand story with customers.

ENSURE THAT EMPLOYEES UNDERSTAND HOW TO CREATE WE RELATIONSHIPS

First, you must help the employees in your organization *understand* how to create We relationships. Share with them the idea of encounters vs. transactions, and explain the three elements of an encounter, as described in Chapter 2. I have found that the ideas described in this book, especially those related to creating We encounters, are both attractive and accessible concepts for employees of all levels.

You may want to use language that is appropriate and relevant to your organization's culture. For example, in our work with Kimpton Hotels implementing the concepts in this book, we have described an encounter between a guest and an employee as a "Kimpton Moment." As you can see from the materials on the following page, excerpted from our workshops with Kimpton employees, a Kimpton Moment follows the definition and structure of relationship-building encounters, as have been described in this book.

We developed these workshops to involve employees in discussions of Kimpton Moments, exploring with them how people in their particular job role create relationship-building encounters.

My experience has always been that highly participative and interactive training sessions yield creative ideas from those being trained, and the Kimpton workshops reinforced that experience. Earlier (page 46) I mentioned an insight from Carlo Stuart, of Kimpton's Hotel Allegro in Chicago, in which he described being engaged in the moment with a customer as "being loyal to that customer." That was one of the freshest comments I have heard about customer loyalty since the invention of the frequent flyer program.

On the subject of treating people like unique human beings, Reggie Griffith, bell captain at the Kimpton's Hotel Burnham in Chicago said, "We need to shatter stereotypes about our customers.

THE KIMPTON MOMENT

An encounter with a guest
where our relationship grows stronger.

hotels & restaurants

KIMPTON   *The Kimpton Moment*

A KIMPTON MOMENT HAS 3 ELEMENTS

The Setting-Engagement in the Moment

- Be there in the moment!
- Be fully present and invite the guest to be fully present.

Conversation

- Your job is not only to tell our story. It is to be in dialogue with this guest. This enables both of you to create this guest's personal version of the Kimpton story.

Uniqueness & Authenticity

- Make this a special, authentic encounter between two special, unique people.

hotels & restaurants

KIMPTON   *The Kimpton Moment*

You can't judge a customer by what you see on the surface—that they are a businessman or a businesswoman—and assume things about them. You need to interact with them and read them. Then you can see them for who they are."

Prior to the development of this Kimpton Moment initiative, Kimpton's front desk employees were required to follow a fifteen-step check-in procedure, in which they described each of the hotel's amenities and features. At one point in the development of this initiative, Mike Defrino, senior vice president of operations for Kimpton Hotels, said, "We don't need a fifteen-step check-in procedure, we need one step: Connect with the customer." Bravo, Mike. By focusing on customer engagement and the creation of encounters, it became clear that a rigid, scripted procedure impeded Kimpton Moments. By looking at the list of hotel amenities and features less as a checklist and more as a "toolbox," front desk personnel are able to have conversations with guests about the amenities that are of most interest to that guest.

Employees Understand Customer Relationships through Their Own Relationships with the Company

> Unscripted, empowered employees can create personalized, brand-building encounters.

Earlier I quoted Niki Leondakis, Kimpton's chief operating officer, describing how unscripted, empowered employees can create personalized, brand-building encounters. Niki believes that one of the best ways to help employees believe this is by how you treat them on the job. "I firmly believe that personalizing their employment experience is the best way to get them to personalize the guest experience. I absolutely, firmly believe that. When they come to work every day, and all day long they're treated like and feel like an individual, then they will treat guests that way."

We Relationships Must Be Central to the Company's Internal Culture

With 6,000 employees it is a tall order, but individualism is so ingrained in Kimpton's culture that it's easy for employees to understand. Reggie Griffith, the Kimpton bell captain we met earlier, adds, "We always walk in to the job as who we are." Other Kimpton employees reiterated this sentiment, saying things such as "They recruited us for who we were," "Anybody can hire robots, they want individuals," "We interact with each other as individuals, not stiff and rigid," and "We're supposed to own the moment and let our personality come through." The way your employees feel you treat them will naturally be reflected in the way they treat customers. If employees feel a good, strong We relationship with your company, they will be more likely to understand how to create We relationships with customers.

Doug Ducey of Cold Stone Creamery agrees that the way customers are related to is a reflection of what happens inside the company. He describes how he sees this at Cold Stone Creamery. "It would be easy for me to create 'We' with customers if I were on the front line, but I'm not. With 1350 stores, I can't be. But I can ask 'Are we bringing on franchisees who understand what engagement means, and the commitment it takes?' If we do, we'll have that spirit in our stores, and it will be easier to bring that spirit out in the young teenagers who work for us. It's very achievable to do that. Then I think you get much closer to 'We.'"

Employees of all levels learn what is important to their organization from cultural cues they witness while on the job. If the idea of strong customer relationships is hardly ever mentioned within an organization, it wouldn't be surprising if creating strong customer relationships wasn't high on employees' personal lists of priorities. Of course, some relationship building will happen naturally, but, even in those cases, it will seem to those employees like a pleasant addition to their work experience as opposed to a core element of their job.

On the other hand, if strong customer relationships are discussed constantly as a central focus of the organization, if employees see senior executives focusing on building strong customer

> If the company's reward structure favors people who create strong customer relationships, employees will focus on creating strong customer relationships.

relationships, and if the company's reward structure favors people who create strong customer relationships, employees will focus on creating strong customer relationships.

When we remember that creating strong relationships in a business setting calls on the same skills and abilities that help us create strong personal relationships, we can see how simple this should be. The first thing we should do is get out of employees' way, and show them an environment where strong relationships are appreciated. Then, we can describe the specific kinds of encounters and relationships that the company is trying to create, as we did with the Kimpton Moments example. Employees will not resist this. On the contrary, it will make work seem more familiar and more like real life than the regimented, bureaucratic situations they've probably worked in previously.

ENSURE THAT EMPLOYEES CAN CREATE WE RELATIONSHIPS

Had Kimpton Hotels not abandoned the check-in script, it would have been difficult for front desk personnel to create Kimpton Moment encounters, no matter how well they understood the concept. To make it possible for your organization to create We relationships with customers, it is important to eliminate obstacles that prevent employees from creating We relationships.

> Obstacles may be in the form of rules, operational constraints, or inadequate resources.

These obstacles may be in the form of rules, operational constraints, or inadequate resources.

Rule obstacles are policies or procedures that dictate employee behavior that makes it difficult for employees to create encounters and, subsequently, relationships. Scripts, like those mentioned above, fall into this category because they prevent uniqueness. Performance measures that

> **The important issue is whether you will deliberately prioritize your efforts to make it easier for people in your organization to create We relationships.**

encourage employees to finish conversations quickly, which are often found in call centers, may have short-term economic merit, but they can limit an employee's ability to engage a customer in the moment and create a conversation.

Operational constraints prevent encounters by limiting employee capabilities. Among the most common are computer constraints that make it difficult for employees to access customer information that supports unique encounters. There are many companies that track important, non-confidential information about customers, such as purchase history, but they don't make it readily available to employees during customer interactions. For example, many hotel companies collect customer preference data, but this data is cumbersome for reservationists to access during the booking process. Similarly, many companies have operational processes that inhibit encounters, such as automated telephone call prompting or reporting systems that don't immediately alert salespeople to problems their customers may be having.

Resource limitations are critical, not only because they can inhibit employees' abilities to create encounters, but because they can be expensive to address. In many cases, We encounters sometimes (but not always) take longer than transactions, requiring more manpower. The decision to allocate more employee time to customer interactions is one that is not taken lightly, since adding "headcount" is, for most companies, an important investment decision.

Many of these obstacles cannot be easily eradicated; many are expensive to address, and they are often embedded deep in a company's operational systems. However, it is possible to eliminate many of them. The important issue is whether you are willing to deliberately prioritize your efforts on operational enhancements that make it easier for people in your organization to create We relationships. For example, imagine that your company has two constraints in its information technology systems, but can only afford to address one of these problems at this time. The first requires accounts payable clerks to double-enter certain pieces of information on invoices. The second makes it cumbersome for customer service employees to access unique information about customers' purchase preferences on a telephone call. Assume both problems cause the same amount of employee hassle and both problems cost the same to fix. Which will your company address? It should address the second issue, which makes it difficult for customer service people to create unique encounters with customers.

In my experience, these types of decisions are usually not made with the customer relationship in mind. Usually, the position of the person in the company who is asking for change is considered more important than how customer interactions will be affected. Senior managers, who are also good salespeople for their projects, are usually those whose operational constraints are addressed first.

Another obstacle that makes it difficult for employees to engage in relationship-building We encounters with customers is the technical demands of their job. Rob Lemen, the Starbucks manager mentioned earlier, says this: "My theory is that people are less likely to engage with customers if they're not feeling confident about what they're doing. So it's my job on the front end when somebody starts working with us to give them all the tools they need to succeed and give them really thorough training. I first want to make sure that they really have a solid foundation on how to use the register system and make drinks. When they're confident doing the basics of the operation, then that frees up their mind to engage with the customers. When it becomes like riding a bike—when you can do it as second nature—then you can focus on talking with customers."

I then asked Rob if he thinks engaging with customers takes longer, making it difficult for employees to serve customers in a timely manner. "No, you can do it really quickly. If I'm on the register, I will get to the business at hand first, "Hey, Good morning. What can I get for you?" They'll give me their order and I'll start ringing it up, and as I'm ringing it up I'll say 'So, how's your day going today? What are you up to?' Stuff like that. It's just a really quick thing but it puts

> I asked if engaging conversation was at odds with giving fast, efficient service. "No way," a Cold Stone employee responded.

personality into the transaction as opposed to 'Here's your change. Next!'"

In my work with Cold Stone Creamery, I had the opportunity to conduct a number of focus groups with their store employees, most of whom were very impressive high school students. In group after group, employees described how their most successful customer interactions happen when they engage customers in good conversation. I asked if engaging conversation was at odds with giving fast, efficient service. "No way," a Cold Stone employee responded. "First off, we're not going to talk for a long time if there's a line or if a customer is in a hurry. But anyway, it usually goes quicker if you get in a conversation with a customer because you can help them figure out what they want." The interaction she described can never happen with a scripted monologue. It is also more difficult if the employee is distracted by the operational demands of his job. Rob Lemen echoes this. "You can engage customers in conversation to help them find what they want if they're confused. And you can move fast and make it happen quickly, but still engage. Even if that engagement is just a minute-and-a-half or even 30 seconds you can still put personality into every transaction."

Steve Pinetti, the senior vice president of marketing and sales for Kimpton Hotels & Restaurants quoted above in chapters 2 and 4, is also the owner of a restaurant, Puccini and Pinetti's, located next to Kimpton's Hotel Monticello in San Francisco. He and I were discussing how important it is to make sure that employees can engage with customers, even if you have to "shore up" technical deficiencies. "I've got some waiters and waitresses who are very efficient. They work quickly and never make a mistake. I have other people who are the best at connecting with and understanding the customer, but they sometimes get carried away and forget some of the details and mechanics that go into serving a meal. I love those people, though. Those are the people who serve lunch to a customer who will then come back for dinner. I can back them up and cover the mechanics, but you can't always make up for a missing emotional connection. It can't be backed up."

TRY THIS>> Look at your company's list of needed operational enhancements. (If you don't have a list, poll your colleagues. Creating a list of necessary "fixes" won't take long.) Look at how the list is prioritized. Are problems that affect encounters with customers at the top of the list, or are they scattered throughout? What are the main factors determining the order of items on the list? Now, redraw the list by giving priority to those problems that create the most obstacles to customer engagement. If you re-prioritized the list in this way, and focused on enhancements that ensure better customer encounters, would you have better relationships with your customers?

MANY OF THEM, MANY OF YOU

The examples we have discussed in this chapter illustrate how a single customer's encounters with people throughout an organization can help that customer have an overall feeling of We with the entire organization. How to engender this feeling in a customer is explained by Brand Harmony; a customer's impression of an organization is created by the way all interactions with that organization blend in his mind to create a composite story.

> A strong We relationship between organizations is built by encounters in the same way a strong personal friendship between two people is built on encounters.

Many relationships, however, involve more than one person on the customer side. A jeweler helping a couple pick out wedding bands, an architect working with a school's building committee, a lawyer working with multiple executives in a client company—in each of these cases the impressions and beliefs of the multiple individuals in the customer organization are critical to the strength of the overall relationship.

These relationships could include multiple people on the seller side, also. The jeweler may bring in the store owner to help with the sale, the school's building committee may be working

> If the relationship between your organizations is built on multiple We relationships between people from both organizations, the relationship will be able to withstand the inevitable personnel changes that will happen.

with a number of people at the architectural firm, and the lawyer may bring a number of his colleagues in to help with this client.

There are no curve balls coming at you in this step: Encounters are the building blocks of We relationships, and a strong We relationship between organizations is built by encounters in the same way a strong personal friendship between two people is built on encounters.

The only difference is that it's harder to make it happen when many people are involved. At an early age we all noticed a phenomenon of human social life—things get exponentially more complicated as more people are added to a situation. (Can't we all remember a time from childhood where we were playing nicely with a friend, and once a third kid showed up the entire chemistry changed, and at least one of us ended up crying?)

To overcome this challenge, be deliberate. With your team, define the kind of We relationship you want to have with this customer, and identify the individual people in the customer organization with whom you want to create We relationships.

If everyone on your team has a shared understanding of the We relationships you are trying to create, as was discussed in the previous section, and you use that understanding to create multiple We relationships within your customer's organization, you will create a strong We relationship between the two organizations.

If the relationship between your organizations is built on multiple We relationships between people from both organizations, the relationship will be able to withstand the inevitable personnel changes that will happen. This chapter started by comparing two scenarios in which a salesperson leaves a company. In one scenario the salesperson is the only person in his company who has a relationship with a particular customer. In the other scenario, multiple people in the salesperson's company have relationships with the customer. Clearly, the customer relationship is more likely to continue in the second scenario.

CONCLUSION: WE—THE BENEFITS ENDURE

OUR SHARED FUTURE—WHAT'S NEXT MATTERS AS MUCH AS WHAT IS

Imagine your customer at some point in the future, say three years from now. Are you a part of that future?

This is one of the most important and tangible dividends from creating We relationships: You will make the future more predictable and more profitable.

As you create a strong We relationship with a customer, one of the most important dividends you will reap is a certain, shared future with that customer.

In a bad relationship, you share only the past. In a strong We relationship, you share not only the past, but the present and the future.

Throughout this book, we have described the technique of "bringing the future forward" a number of times, engaging a customer in the moment by helping him imagine a situation happening sometime in the future. Now, in the context of a strong We relationship, we do not have to bring the future forward; it comes of its own accord. Clarity about "our future together" appears automatically before both you and your customer as your We relationship develops.

This is one of the most important and tangible dividends from creating We relationships: You will make the future more predictable and more profitable. Us & Them customers are fickle; if a new option appears costing only pennies less, they may abandon you without warning. However, as we saw in our research described in Chapter 1, both buyers and sellers prefer to make decisions based on a relationship, not only on price. Your investments in We relationships will pay off in powerful ways, with their benefits accumulating over time as you build a portfolio of strong relationships.

We. A better way to do business. A better way to live.

ACKNOWLEDGMENTS

Writing this book was a We experience. I had the opportunity to collaborate, brainstorm, discuss and revise the idea of the We Customer Relationship with many people, all of whom inspired and energized me. Thanks to...

My wife, Arna, is and always will be the first person I acknowledge when something goes well. In addition to everything else wonderful about Arna, she is an excellent editor and is the whispering navigator behind everything I write.

Caroline Ceisel, my associate at Yastrow Marketing, has lived with this book from its inception, and contributed everything from guiding details to blockbuster insights. Kenzi and Kenichi Sugihara at SelectBooks have made both of my books a reality. Kenzi is the true We publisher, and proof that We collaboration works.

Other colleagues contributed in significant ways to the content and text of the book. Cathy Mosca's editing help was not only precise and insightful, but creative and poetic. Amanda Kinslow's editing help midway through the project was invaluable in getting the book ready for the final phase of writing. Steve Elliott, of Steve Elliott Marketing Research, is my market research oracle, and his help with the research in Chapter 1 was invaluable. Janice Benight for the elegant–and readable–page design.

Many thanks to...

My family–in addition to my wife/editor Arna, my kids Nurit, Levi and Noah, my parents Sybil and Shelby, my siblings Phil and Sara and their spouses Ellen and Bob, my father-in-law Ben Sosewitz, and Ethel and Paul Pickar, all of whom are a continuous and nurturing source of guidance and support. Phil and I carry on the ultimate ongoing conversation; Chapter 3 is dedicated to him.

My writing partners, David Gottlieb and Karyn Kedar, whose inspiration and voices inform all of my creative thoughts. Karyn's husband, my close friend Ezra, who sees language in a way no one else can. My long-time close friends and musical creative partners, Chuck and Rachel Rosenberg. Our band's 3rd CD, featuring my son Levi, has just been released...it's been a creative year! Brian Kovach, my colleague of 20 years, who plays the role of friend, near-brother, strategic partner, brainstormer, life-support system, bass player and lead singer in a way nobody else could, has his fingerprint on everything I do.

And...Tom Peters, Erik Hansen and Cathy Mosca (encore) at Tom Peters Company for their ongoing support.

My friends and clients at Kimpton Hotels-Niki Leondakis, Steve Pinetti, Holly Houston, Mike Depatie, Nir Margalit and Renee Will George—provided valuable insight, support and inspiration. As described in this book, our work on "The Kimpton Moment" was inter-dependent with my work on We, and my collaboration with the Kimpton team helped crystallized this idea.

Thanks to Todd Knutson and Brandon Doty at The List, Inc. in Atlanta for collaborating with me on the research in Chapter 1. Doug Ducey and Kevin Myers at Cold Stone Creamery for support, friend-ship and ideas.

This book gave me an excuse to engage in many wonderful con-versations, many of which resulted in direct quotes in the text, some of which were just as valuable for their inspiration. The timing of some was uncanny. I'll never forget running into my friend David Chack on a flight at 30,000 feet over the Mediterranean shortly after starting the book. I learned of David's expertise in Martin Buber, and filled up all sides of three air sickness bags furiously taking notes as David related Buber stories he had learned as Nahum Glatzer's last grad-uate assistant.

Many other serendipitous conversations surprised me at oppor-tune times with instant inspiration: Chuckie Edelson, my wife's uncle, at Moshav Orot in Israel; meeting up with my good friend David Baker in Jerusalem, where we had some formative conversations about We relationships at coffee shop T'mol Shilshom; Rob Lemen of Starbucks in San Francisco, at 6:15 in the morning; Mike Gelbort over appetizers at a bar mitzva reception; meeting Alberto Was from Uruguay, a distant cousin my wife, at Kibbutz Kfar Blum in Israel; renowned psychologist and author Hendrie Weisinger sitting at the next table in a hotel restaurant in Cleveland, both of us in town for speeches the next day; Dr. Jay Ferraro at a conference in Rhode Island; Joe Honor at a 4th of July picnic; more than a few late night discussions with Neal Kusnetz; Einat Amitai at T'mol Shilshom in

Jerusalem, all of these people proved the value of being open to encounter. You never know it when it may find you. Be ready.

And to my other insightful interviewees: Alan Malmed, Roz Alexander, Stuart Rosenberg, Mike Konopka, Jai Luster, Miriam Clarke, Chris Anderson, Doug Stevenson, Rob Shell, Charles Dann, and Stuart Hershkowitz.

Also...The folks at Silverware in Scottsdale for keeping yastrow. com alive.

Others who have contributed to the success of Yastrow Marketing: Carol Chalfant, Michelle Adderly, Diana Lackner and Lynn Harris. And to Jim Harris, to whom I can trace the genealogy of so many of my ideas...and clients. Devlin Driscoll. My partners at Lighthouse Carwash—Norm Siegel, Mike Kinslow, Woody Black and Pat Sherman. Ramon Abarca of Rhapsody Café in Deerfield, IL, for demonstrating the premium value of a "We omelette" vs. the Us & Them variety found elsewhere.

INDEX

A

Aboutism, 63–69. *See also* Present moment

avoidance. *See* Customers

Abundance, belief, 183

Acknowledgment, importance, 68–69

Actions. *See* Complementary actions

usage, 160–161

Advertising-based beliefs, limitation, 10

Alertness. *See* Present moment

Alexander, Roslyn, 52, 91

Anderson, Chris, 9, 104–111

filtering, perspective, 110–111

Apple Computer, 8

B

Baker, David, 180

Barnes & Noble, 9

Being present. *See* Present moment

Be the Brand, 188–189

occurrence, 189

Blockbuster Video, 89

Brand

being (Be the Brand), 188–189

creation, opportunity, 24

essence, identification, 67–68

harmony, concept, 189

impression, 24–25

employees, impact. *See* Customers

formation, 143

perception, 22–27

strategy. *See* We

Brand Harmony (Yastrow), 3, 24, 188

concept, 189

Bridge moments, 144

usage. *See* Milestone moments

Bridge to Forgiveness (Kedar), 63
British Airways, technology (usage), 7
Brute force (marketing/branding
    method), 168
Buber, Martin, 12, 30, 33, 55, 69, 73, 114
    biography, 98–99
    lesson. *See* Customer relationships

C
Categorization. *See* People
Ceisel, Caroline (collaboration), 14
Characteristics, sharing, 162
Clarity/alertness, 87–88
Clarke, Miriam, 165
Cold Stone Creamery
    customers, relation, 193
    focus groups, 197
    relationship, belief, 17
Collaboration
    importance, 178–179
    usage, 180–181
Collaborative filtering, 109
Coltrane, John, 89
Commerce, change, 5
Companies
    customer
        care, perception, 22–23
        relationships, importance, 23
    employee relationships, 192
    identity, defining, 67–68
    impact. *See* Customers
    internal culture, We relationships
        (importance), 193–194
    measurements, 4
    messages, expenditures, 168
    policies, impact, 95–96
    recommendation, pattern, 15
Company-wide memory, 130–131
Competition, complement (transition),
    158–159

Competitors, copying (limitation), 5
Complement
    impact. *See* Relationships
    process, 158
    revelation, encounter continuity
        (usage), 159–160
Complementary actions, 177–181
    opportunities, 179–181
    relationships, evolution, 180
    We encounter, relationship, 177–178
Complementary goals, 170–177
    revelation, 177
Complementary outcomes, 181–183
    meaning, 182
Complementary understanding,
    160–161
        relation, 161–170
        revelation, 169–170
Conscious awareness, 128
Consistency, overrating, 93
Contextual listening, 59
Continual conversations, continuous
    conversations (contrast), 148–149
Continuity, development, 124, 157
Conversation
    alertness/adjustment, 84
    contrast. *See* Continual
        conversations
    encounter element, 41
    explanation, 73–88
    extraction, 45–46
    forcing, avoidance. *See* Customers
    imbalance, management, 84–85
    importance, Kedar example, 81
    moment, element, 191
    paths, 81–83
    qualities, 87
    shared story, emergence. *See* On-
        going conversation
    tracking, 83–84

Corante, 107
Costco, benefit, 182
Crosbie, Vin, 107
CSI: Crime Scene Investigation, 106
Customer-driven trends, evolution, 3
Customer Relationship Management
 Systems (CRM), 5, 130
Customer relationships. See Executives
 Buber, lesson, 32–33
 emergence, 135–136
 support, technology (usage), 8
Customers
 aboutism, avoidance, 65–69
 abstractions/statistics, conversion, 101
 actions, 25–27
  likelihood, 26
  taking, 141–142
 avoidance, technology (usage), 6
 beliefs, 24–25
 boundaries, 11
 brand impression, employees
  (impact), 188–189
 characteristics, recognition, 166–167
 conversation, forcing (avoidance),
  81–82
 co-subjects, 112–113
 definition, 27–28
 depersonalization, companies
  (impact), 10
 desirability, belief, 19
 encounters
  importance, 198–200
 encounters, consideration, 72
 engagement, 49
  importance, 197–198
 feelings/thoughts, 118–119
 goals
  discovery, assistance, 173–175
  knowledge, 175–176
  learning, 172–173

identification, 27–28
interactions
 delegation, 6
 employee basis, 93–94
 interests, focus, 132
 invitation. See Present moment
 refusal, reasons, 60–62
 knowledge, recognition, 166–167
 love, 22
 loyalty, 46
 memory, 131–133
 need, niche characteristic, 110–111
 obstacles/barriers, removal
  (challenge), 72
 organization, turnover (challenges),
  20–21
 personal encounter, creation, 97–98
 personal issues, boundaries, 112
 perspectives, executive perceptions
  (inaccuracies), 117–118
 population, division/management,
  100–101
 profitability, perception, 19
 purchases, 2
 recognition, 168–169
 recommendation, perception, 19
 relationships
  employee understanding, 192
  strengthening, 193–194
 segmentation, techniques, 100–101
 success, desire, 170
 We relationship
  creation, 204
  entry, 3–4
 words, encouragement, 68

D
Dance of the Dolphin (Kedar), 63
Dann, Charles, 181
Dell Computer, 8

Delta Partners, encounter example,
141–145
Demographic generalizations, 100–101
Details
    attention. *See* Present moment
    remembering, capacity, 127–128
    sharing, 162–165
        absence, 165–166
    usage, 104
Dialogue. *See* Genuine dialogue;
    Technical dialogue
    types, 76–77
    words, 79
Dialogue (Buber), 73
DNA, percent shared, 103
Ducey, Doug
    customers, relation process, 193
    relationships, 11
    service-based economy, 28
    Us/Them perspective, 71

E
Elevator pitch, uselessness, 77–78
Elliott, Steve (collaboration), 14
Empathy/engagement, 68–69
Employees
    ability. *See* We relationships
    customer engagement, importance,
        197–198
    empowerment, customer
        perception, 95
    encouragement. *See* We encounters
    impact. *See* Customers
    policy, constraints, 94
    relationships. *See* Companies
    technical demands, obstacles,
        196–197
    training, problems, 93
    understanding. *See* Customers;
        We relationships

Encounters, 39–40. *See also* We encounters
    bonds, 125–126
    building blocks. *See* We relationships
    continuity, 124, 147–153
        usage. *See* Complement
    creation, 137–139
        overview, 113–114
        problems, 139–140
        process, 99
        techniques, 151–152
    definition, 39
    distraction, avoidance. *See* Pre-
        sent moment
    elements, 41. *See also* We
    freshness, 89–90
    frictionless interaction, 70–71
    interest, usage, 101–102
    invention, 89
    irreplaceability, 97–115
    memorability, process, 131–133
    memory, connection, 125–134
    number, selection, 139–140
    pace, planning, 140
    preparatory mindset, 43
    process. *See* Human encounter
    relationship, 40
    rhythm, 134–140
    series, creation, 145
    setting, 42
    success, 57
    uniqueness, 91–92
    we relationship building blocks, 37
Engagement. *See* Empathy/engagement;
    Present moment
    dynamic condition, 34
    human connection, 33
    obstacles, media (impact), 69–73
    transition. *See* Experience/engagement
Engagement in the moment

encounter element, 41
explanation, 41–73
Experience Economy, The (Pine & Gilmore), 32
Experience/engagement, transition, 32–34
Eye contact, presence (communication), 58–59

F

Ferraro, Jay, 33, 59, 74, 158
Filtering. *See* Collaborative filtering
perspective, 110–111
Filters. *See* Long tail
Fisher, Dr. Elisa Barak, 73–74
Freshness. *See* Encounters; Improvisation
cessation, repetition (impact), 89–93
Frictionless conversation, 75
Friedman, Maurice, 98–99
Future
bring forward, 65–67

G

Gelbort, Michael, 125–129
Generalizations. *See* Demographic generalizations
Genuine dialogue, 76
requirement, 84–85
Goals. *See* Complementary goals
approach/work, 178
discovery, assistance. *See* Customers
identification, 174
learning. *See* Customers
usage, 160–161. *See also* Shared story
God Whispers (Kedar), 63
Grant, Cary, 84
Griffith, Reggie, 193

H

Hepburn, Katherine, 84
Hershkowitz, Stuart, 111–113
Hit culture, development, 104–105
Honor, Joe
conversation example, 82–83
interruption, example, 174–175
Human beings
fullness, 103–104, 111, 113–114
relationships, reward, 30
uniqueness, belief, 98–102
Human encounter, process, 101
Human interaction, power, 124–125
Humor, usage, 61–62

I

I and Thou (Buber), 12, 30, 69
I/It relationship, 30–31
Improvisation
freshness, 89–90
process, 53. *See also* Stage improvisation
Interdependency, impact, 178–179
Invitation
customers, 57
obstacles, media (impact), 69–73
possibility, presence (impact). *See* Present moment
refusal, reasons. *See* Customers; Present moment
Irreplaceability. *See* Encounters
process, 98
I/Thou
idea, 30–32
relationship, 31–32

J

Joint teams, opportunities, 179–181

K

Kedar, Karyn, 63
    conversation, tracking, 81, 83–84
Kimpton Hotels & Restaurants
    customer
        perspective, 78
        research, 16, 17
        value, 94
    employees, customer engagement
        (importance), 197–198
    moment, elements, 191
    present moment, survey, 46
Kovach, Brian, 180
Kusnetz, Neal, 144–145

L

Lemen, Rob, 61, 196–197
Lenscrafters, 124
Leondakis, Niki, 94–95, 192
Life relationships, reflection, 147–148
List, Inc., The, 18
Listening. *See* Contextual listening
    importance. *See* Present moment
    usage, 59–60
Long tail
    distribution curve, 105–106
    filters, 109–111
    individuality, relationship, 104–109
    phenomenon, 107
Long Tail, The (Anderson), 9, 104, 111

M

Malmed, Alan, 58
Marketing. *See* Word of mouth marketing
    impact. *See* Seller/customer distance
    instruction, problems, 28–30
    life, comparison, 29–30
    metaphor, 74
    technologies, direct
        communication, 70

    usage. *See* Storytelling
Mass advertising, effectiveness
    (continuation), 106–107
Media
    impact. *See* Engagement; Invitation
    necessity, 70
Memories
    determination, 127–128
    uniqueness, impact, 133
Memory. *See* Company-wide memory;
    Customers
    connection between encounters,
        125–126
    consolidation, sleep (impact), 129–130
    development, 137–139
    durability, 126–127
    palpability, 126–127
    strategies, 128
Metaphors, selection, 132
Milestone moments, 140–144
    bridge moments, usage, 144–146
    identification, 143–144
Miscommunication (Mortenson), 153
Moments. *See* Bridge moments;
    Milestone
    moments
    mixture, 140–147
Monological storytelling, 75
Monologue
    creation, care, 62
    dialogue
        conversion, 75
        disguise, 76–77
        tendency, avoidance, 85
    words, 79
Multi-modal inputs, receiving, 127
Mutual self-recognition, 169–170

N

Netflix, 9, 105

Niche
    narrowness, 107–108
    portfolios, 108
Non-business characteristics,
    commonality, 163–164
Now, value, 43–45

O

Observation/response. *See* Present
    moment
Obstacles. *See* Rule obstacles
    removal, challenge. *See* Customers
Ongoing conversation
    appearance, 152–153
    explanation, 124–153
    shared story, emergence, 149–151
Operational constraints, impact,
    194, 195
Operational enhancements, efforts,
    195–196
Organizations
    challenges, 21
    relationships, 187
        We relationships, dependence,
        199–200
    We relationships, creation, 188–189
Outcome, 160–161. *See also* Comple-
    mentary outcomes
    abundance, 183
    anxiety, avoidance, 56
Outsourcing, opportunities, 179–181

P

Pause, usage. *See* Present moment
Pendragon, Ron, 165
People
    categorization, 99–100
    complementary goals, perception,
        177
    conversation, assistance, 86

interaction, ability, 114–115
interest, 52
learning context, 133
observations, limitlessness, 114
real life examples, 102
relationship, development, 163–164
specialization, 165–166
stories, creation, 117
uniqueness, 161–162
    cues, 103–104
Personal encounter, creation. *See*
    Customers
Personal life, relationships (creation),
    29–30
Perspective, usage, 115–118
Perspicuity/perspicacity, 87–88
Pessl, Marisha, 75
Philadelphia Story, The, 84
Pinetti, Steve, 78, 170, 197–198
Ping, usefulness, 146–147
Power of Now, The (Tolle), 50
Preparatory mindset. *See* Encounters
Presence, communication. *See* Eye
    contact
Present moment (being present), 45–46
    aboutism, 63–64
    alertness, 50–51
    attention, 42–43
    customers, invitation, 57–58
    details, attention, 50–51
    encounter, distraction (avoidance),
        55–57
    entry, strategy, 49–50
    investment, 51–52
    invitation
        possibility, presence (impact),
            58–59
        refusal, nonrealization, 63
        refusal, reasons, 60–62
    listening, importance, 59–60

observation/response, 52–53
pause, usage, 48–49
resistance, 54–55
strategies, 46–47
uniqueness, alertness, 91
Price, importance, 15
Products, features (importance), 23–24
Progress, impact, 5–10

Q
Quality time, focus, 136–137

R
Reference, frame, 4–5
Relationship-building encounters,
37–120
Relationship-building strategy, focus, 111
Relationships
belief, 16
change, 4
conversation, continuity, 145–146
creation, 3–4. See also Personal life
conversation, contribution, 148
importance, 10
customer belief, 142–143
differentiators, 3
early stage, 151
evolution, 11. See also
Complementary
actions
formation, 124
frustration, 10
importance, 16–17
inclusion, 198–199
measurements, 4
momentum, building, 134–140
pace, creation, 135
personality, complement (impact),
159
quality, 115

reward. See Human beings
story, creation, 143–144
success, identification, 140–141
support, technology (usage). See
Customers
tangibility, 181–182
Remembering, 128–130
determination, 127–128
Repetition
impact. See Freshness
usefulness, 90–93
Reporting, 63, 68
Resources, inadequacy/limitations,
194, 195
Results, goals (relationship), 181
Retail selling, dynamic, 44–45
Rhapsody (online music retailer), 105
Rhythm, of encounters, 134–136
Robert Graham, Inc., 144
Rosenberg, Stuart (future, discussion),
59, 66, 72
Rule obstacles, 194–195

S
Salespeople, relationship scenarios, 188
Sales philosophies, impact, 150
Self-interest, genuineness, 171–172
Self-knowledge, 161–170
Self-recognition. See Mutual self-
recognition
Seller/customer distance, marketing
(impact), 71
Sensitivity, 118–119
Setting-engagement, moment element,
191
Shared future, importance, 204
Shared story
continuation, 152
creation, 151–152
emergence. See Ongoing conversation

goals, usage, 176–177
  idea, 149
Shared understanding, creation, 65
Shell, Rob, 179–180
Signal to noise ratio, 110
Silver, Sara, 163–164
Silverware, Inc., 163
Sim lev, 51
Socrates, lessons, 80–81
South Haven, Michigan, 92
Spontaneity, feeling, 89–90
Springsteen, Bruce, 164
Stage improvisation, process, 54
Starbucks, 61
Stern, Lisa, 164
Stevenson, Doug, 62, 131–132
Storytelling, 62
  marketing, usage, 74–88
Stuart, Carlo, 46
Success
  interest, 170–172
  picture, 141
  tracing, actions (impact), 183

T
Tacking, 83–84
Tangible results, impact, 181–182
Targeting, cessation, 78–79
Teamwork, meaning, 178
Technical dialogue, 76
Technology
  choices, problems, 9–10
  impact, 6
  investment, 7
  usage. See Customer relationships
    choice, 6–7
    examples, 6–8
Time allocation, challenges, 22
Tolle, Eckhard, 50
Tomorrow, preparation, 43

Touchpoints, examination, 72–73
Tower Records, 9
Training sessions, participation/
  interaction, 190
Transactions, 38
  definition, 39
  relationship, 40

U
Uniqueness. See Encounters
  alertness, 91
  belief, 114
  connection, 161–162
  cues. See People
  encounter element, 41, 108
  explanation, 89–119
  interference, process (impact),
    93–96
  moment element, 191
  policy, impact, 93
Us/Them, contrast. See We
Us/Them relationships, 11
  benefits, derivation (possibility), 182
  change, 4
  contrast. See We relationships

V
Validation, importance, 68–69

W
Wal-Mart, 105
Was, Alberto, 166–167
We
  brand strategy, 22–27
  business relationship, 171
  consideration, 2–3
  crossroads, 41
  feeling, attempt, 2–3
  profitability, 12–22
  question, 1

Us/Them, contrast, 11–12
value, 12–14
We encounters, 109–111
creation, employees (encouragement), 189–190
elements, 41
relationship. *See* Complementary
actions
Weisinger, Hendrie, 171
Weiss, Alan, 174
We relationships, 11–12
change, 4
comparison. *See* Collaborative relationship
creation. *See* Customers
challenges, 20
employee ability, 194–198
employee understanding,
190–194
encounters, building blocks, 199
importance. *See* Companies
life, improvement, 12–22
mutual direction, 28
success, aspect, 115–116
Us/Them relationship, contrast,
13, 182
When, importance, 136–137
With, feeling of, 120
Word of mouth marketing, 70–71
Words
assistance, 86
encouragement. *See* Customers
usage, 67–68

Y
Yastrow Marketing, research, 188
Yes, and (stage technique), 54
usage, 81–83